Sally Butcher

New
Middle Eastern
Street Food

Snacks, Comfort Food, and Mezze from Snackistan

INTERLINK BOOKS
an imprint of Interlink Publishing Group, Inc.
www.interlinkbooks.com

For Afi, for unlocking the doors of the
Persian kitchen for me. And for Baba, for
keeping our little Persian empire together.
As in-laws go, they ain't bad.

contents .

Introduction

Snackistan: a slightly East-of-center, fictitious land where tummies are always full, and there's a slightly naughty smile on every face. Snackistan does not, of course, exist, any more than Veggiestan does. It is, rather, a borderless confederation of the Middle East's favorite foodstuffs. The simple fare that people eat on a daily basis: dishes they prepare at home, or cook to share with friends, or look forward to indulging in at the end of the week; the food of choice across the region.

We all like to snack. This is, I suspect, because the concept goes against everything that parents, followed by newspapers and dieticians, have hitherto told us: "don't eat between meals," eating in the street is "vulgar/bad for the digestion," "you'll spoil your appetite"… I personally still feel a little frisson of rebelliousness every time I dig into an unscheduled portion of fries/spontaneous ice cream.

And yet snacking comes so naturally to us. By which I don't mean that we're all Homer-Simpson-esque rampant gluttons. Rather that, with our busy lifestyles, we are all becoming grazers, and most medical professionals now endorse this by concluding that eating "little and often" is better for our poor overloaded digestive systems. The Iranians have a proverb for this: Eat little and sleep sound. They also have another apt saying: Eat little, always eat. Snacking may actually be better for your wallet too.

Increasingly, formal dining is being nudged aside in favor of *mezze*-style spreads: samples of a wide range of (often simple) foods, shared in leisurely fashion.

At the same time, street food has come of age (although street-cart doner kebabs are still a dire alternative to food). In malls and farmers' markets across the land, food on the hoof has become a stylish and popular way to eat: sandwiches are getting a big makeover, savory pies are back in vogue, and even Chinese takeout is now as likely to have been cooked in front of you in a mobile wok as assembled secretly behind a door that always remains suspiciously closed.

Origins of street food and *mezze*

It hardly needs pointing out that both *mezze* and in all likelihood street food vending originated in the area I have now labeled Snackistan. (It does need pointing out, however, before you question my geography, that I have deliberately wobbled over the edges of the area conventionally known as the Middle East, straying into neighboring Greece and Sudan, for example.) Street food is far from a recent innovation: as far back as the Classical age, Greek and Roman writers alluded to open-air food vendors in the Mediterranean, and it is apparent that during times when not everyone had an oven or even a kitchen at home, there was a burgeoning market for such fare. This early takeout was popular too with travelers, for whom it was often the only food option available. But it was in medieval times that demand seems to have surged, and busy cities such as Cairo boasted an impressive array of specialized food vendors (collectively known as *tabbakhun*; it is fun to think that the little store I run with my husband qualifies for the description as well, although I am not sure it will catch on) ranging from *halwaniyyun* (literally *halva* sellers) to *haraisiyyun*, who hawked *harisseh* (or *halim*: see p.74). In Turkey in the Middle Ages, takeout kebabs were becoming popular, and Istanbul was already working towards its current position as one of the street-food capitals of the world. Pie stalls and dough-based treats evolved to sate the carb requirements of the poorer classes, many of whom, again, were without a bread oven at home.

Of course, it helps that most of Snackistan enjoys considerably warmer weather than northwestern Europe and many parts of the United States: this coaxes people out of doors and fosters street culture and politics, both of which need feeding. In fact, street food offers a fascinating snapshot of the social development of a nation. This is the case even in the diaspora: a survey of foreign takeout restaurants and popular back-home foods in London, where I live, tells you much about the lands of origin therein. In my home-district of Peckham alone, there are any number of street hawkers: our favorites are the quiet, anxious-looking man who wanders round with steaming boxes of spicy hot Afghan *qorma* in winter and the flamboyant West Indian drink vendor who appears on a bicycle in summer with a huge slab of ice and worryingly brightly-colored syrups.

Street food may have been the poor man's food of antiquity, but *mezze* had altogether grander origins. The word *mezze* (*meze/mezedes*) is derived from *mazeh*, which is the Farsi word for "taste," and the concept as a type of repast almost certainly evolved in the courts and eateries of Iran. The original idea was snippets or tasters of food to be eaten alongside and to mop up *arak*, wine, or beer. It was clearly taken quite seriously, as Rumi refers to it repeatedly in his works, thus: "*Cook mezze from tears on thy heart's fire; field and flower have been debauched by the clouds and the sun.*"

There is a rather wonderful but spurious tale that the whole "taster" thing pertained to the custom among kings (who were undeniably more scandal-ridden and less secure than today's royalty) of having their food tasted lest it was poisoned. The sultans of the Ottoman Empire reputedly adopted the idea and the business of setting out a meal as a series of little platters took off from there. The conversion of much of the region to Islam did not put an end to the unhurried consumption of *mezze* over a few drinks, but in the more devoutly

Muslim (and thus non-drinking) nations it is now more often consumed as a selection of appetizers before a meal. Further west, however, in the Levant and Greece and Turkey, *mezze* thrives as a major feature of the cuisine and a vast range of dishes have been created expressly with that style of eating in mind (many of them by the aforementioned Ottomans).

A celebration of comfort food

We may have become aware of the idea of comfort food and comfort eating only in the last couple of decades, but we have of course been cooking it for millennia: for the most part, it comprises the default dishes prepared by those who need a reminder of home, a culinary hug. The ritual act of preparing such familiar food is undoubtedly as soothing to the cook as it is to those who get to enjoy it. I am in a unique position to observe the phenomena, as my little emporium is located in such a wonderfully cosmopolitan corner of London that there are representatives from every corner of Snackistan and beyond trying to cook up a little bit of back home. The dishes my customers prepare are the stuff of childhood teatimes and family breakfasts, nutritious and usually cheap (a lot of it based on popular Ramadan recipes as there is no stronger focus on food than during the month of fasting).

Snackistan is all about celebrating these less formal styles of eating. It is not about fast food, or fifteen-minute meals, or three-ingredient suppers, and in fact some of the dishes contained within these pages take quite a long time to prepare. My mother-in-law frequently spends a whole day preparing comfort food snacks to sate her clamorous and largely ungrateful brood for the week ahead: fridge food, packed lunch food, busy shopkeeper food... As ever, our friend the wise Mullah Nasruddin illustrates this quite well:

The Mullah was traveling with two acquaintances. After a couple of hours, they stopped by the wayside for a snack, and one of the men pulled out a little bag, announcing, "I only eat roasted and salted pistachios, slivered almonds, and dates. Simple, natural fare."

The second traveler produced a small package. "For me, nothing but the finest dried meat!" he cried.

Clearly it was Nasruddin's turn, and so he removed an old bread crust from his pocket. "Well I only eat ground wheat that has been blended with yeast, sugar, water, and salt and then baked at a certain temperature for the correct amount of time," he informed them...

Nuts and Nibbles

Mullah Nasruddin pretended to be a stern old fellow, but all the neighborhood kids knew that he was a big softee really. Thus when they spotted him buying a big bag of walnuts at the local corner store (okay, market stall), they all ran along behind hoping to cadge some from him.

Allowing them to catch up with him, he generously offered to share his purchase with them.

"But first you must tell me how you would like me to divide the walnuts," said Nasruddin, "The human way or the divine way..."

The boys looked puzzled: whippersnappers they undoubtedly were, but they were God-fearing and well-meaning lads. "Why God's way, of course!" they cried in unison.

The Mullah smiled and reached into the bag. He gave the first boy one walnut, the second a handful of walnuts, the third two handfuls, while the fourth got none.

"You're teasing us, Mullah," said one of the boys. "God wouldn't be that unfair!"

"Ah, well that is where you are wrong. Some of us are born with plenty, some of us born with just enough, and some of us are born without. It is up to us to share things out and look after each other. This is God's little test for us. Now if you'd asked me to share it out the human way: well, you'd all have had equal numbers of nuts."

What the story above illustrates more than anything else is the place of nuts in Snackistan society: as a snack, as an illustration of divine bounty, as a something to offer as a gift, as a form of currency. Yup, nuts are big in the Middle East (no sniggering). Not only is the cuisine liberally studded with nuts of all varieties, they represent what is surely Mother Nature's way of telling us to snack—bite-sized morsels of protein appearing on trees across the countryside on and off throughout the year.

Seeds are also valued snacks, while comprising the sort of stuff we normally throw away/feed to our parrots. Roasted and salted pumpkin, melon, and squash seeds are eaten across the Middle East in HUGE quantities. Hey: one's husband alone eats them in HUGE quantities.

Traditional mini-snacks—nuts and nibbles— remain admirably natural and (oil and salt notwithstanding) for the most part healthy.

That's not to say that people from the Middle East don't also consume junk. Enter any Middle Eastern supermarket in the West and you will encounter aisles of strangely packaged (don't you just love foreign packaging?) sugary and savory snacks. Especially popular are alarmingly yellow cheesy corn puffs (Cheetos by any other name), sweet wafers in five squillion colors and flavors (the Turks are experts at turning these out), breadsticks, sesame treats, and stuffed cookies. And chewing gum, although this can't possibly count as a snack, since you spit it out (discuss)…

Torshi Shoor

AKA MR. SHOPKEEPER'S PATENT PICKLED VEGGIES

Useful Iranian pickle facts: *torshi* in Farsi just means "sour pickle," but is often used as a generic term for pickled things. *Shoor* specifically refers to ingredients preserved predominantly in brine, and *liteh* usually implies a type of finely minced, spicy *torshi*.

These chunky pickled veggies make a great mini-*mezze* dish, since they are effectively pickled crudités. Making anything that you sell in a shop on a regular basis demands a degree of consistency that Mrs. Shopkeeper and her slapdash ways can rarely provide. Mr. Shopkeeper, aka Jamshid, aka my honey bunny, is a much more organized kind of guy than I am. So when it comes to the business of following recipes and doing things in a uniform manner time and again, it is generally understood to be his department. Thus our house pickle, which is enormously popular, is made uniquely by him. This is his secret recipe. Shh—don't tell him I've shared it with you...

It makes enough for at least three jars: one for you, one for the neighbors, and one for the Autumn fair.

* Golpar seeds

That's Persian hogweed to you. It smells like old socks and has a pungent flavor, but works well in pickles. It is also ground and used as a spice in Iran, as it is a "hot" food (Iranians believe that all foods have either "hot" or "cold" properties, and that if you eat too many of one or the other you will end up imbalanced). Put simply, it is sprinkled on lots of "cold" vegetables, such as those served up as snacks in the Iranian bazaars, to reduce the, er, flatulence-inducing effects therein.

FILLS AROUND 3 x 32OZ (1QUART)/800G JARS
2 cauliflowers, separated into small florets
2lb 4oz/1kg carrots, chopped into ½ in/1cm rounds
2 onions, roughly chopped
1 head of celery, cut into ¾ in/2cm lengths
3–4 hot green chilies, chopped
1lb 2oz/500g baby cucumbers, cut into ½–¾ in/1–2cm rounds

6–8 garlic cloves, quartered lengthways
2 tsp whole golpar seeds*
2 tsp whole dill seeds (or use dried dill)
2 level tsp ground turmeric
8 cups/2 liters salted boiled water
generous 2 cups/500ml malt vinegar
1 bunch of fresh spring garlic (or 7oz/200g dried, soaked for 24 hours), optional

This couldn't be easier. Just mix all the ingredients together and ladle into sterilized jars (see below) or a suitable (sterilized) plastic barrel and seal well. Store somewhere cool and dark: your pickles should be ready after about one month.

Sterilizing a jar for this purpose takes two seconds: just fill it with boiling water, sloosh it around and empty it, then leave it upside down somewhere to drain and dry. Sealing a jar is equally straightforward, but if said jar has a metal lid, a little plastic wrap between the product and the lid should prevent an adverse reaction between the two.

Khiar Shoor

PICKLED CUCUMBERS

This is probably the most popular Iranian pickle variety. These posh, pert, and piquant gherkins are nothing short of addictive. In Iran, they are a regular visitor to the dinner table, sliced into sandwiches, chopped into salads, and enjoyed as an any- time snack. Please note they bear about as much resemblance to the burger joint pickle as Pennsylvania to Peckham. They are salty, often eye-wateringly spicy, crunchy, and traditionally very small. In the summer, baby cucumbers can be found in Middle Eastern grocery stores and many supermarkets, so get pickling...

FILLS AROUND 2 x 32OZ
(1QUART)/800G JARS
2lb 4oz/1kg baby cucumbers (about
   1¼ –2½ in/3–6cm in length)
3–4 sprigs of fresh tarragon

4–5 thin, hot chili peppers
4–5 garlic cloves
4 cups/1 liter water with 4 tbsp salt
2 tbsp white vinegar

Wash and drain the cucumbers, tarragon, and chilies, and peel the garlic cloves. Bring the water and salt to a boil, then take off the heat and add the vinegar.

Distribute the cucumbers, chilies, garlic, and tarragon evenly between your sterilized jars (see p.10), cover with the cooled brine, and seal. Store somewhere cool; this delicacy will be ready after a month, but reaches perfection after two.

Who needs chips?

FOUR RECIPES FOR WHEN ONLY
A SALTED SNACK WILL DO

Say snack to most Westerners and nine out of ten* will immediately think of potato chips (or crisps, as we call them here in England). And yet, apart from a quick infusion of salt, they are an unsatisfying munch: they barely fill the tummy for more than 30 minutes and offer few redeeming nutritional features. No, I am not a crisp fan.

Nor am I impressed by the huge amount of unnecessary salt that goes into a lot of our snack food in the West. My husband has me down as a salt-fascist (and keeps what he thinks is a secret emergency stash of the stuff in his office drawer), but I am very pro-salt if it is used wisely. After all, mankind has been gathering and ingesting sodium chloride for tens of thousands of years. If you use moderate amounts of it in your cooking, then you can afford to succumb to the odd craving for an in-your-face salt-fest. Which is what this section is all about: hand-crafted, easy-to-make, mostly healthy, salty treats. The kind they have been eating in the Middle East for centuries. The kind my family-in-law makes all the time at home. Welcome to the Snackistan nut and bean roast…

*I might have invented that statistic.

While we're on the subject of salt…
The citizens of Snackistan do of course eat junk snacks (by which I mean manufactured pre-packaged garbage of no essential nutritional value) aplenty. But there is a range of truly healthy stuff that they render snackable by the simple addition of salt. The kind of stuff that we just don't eat unless it is incorporated into something else, or disguised. When did you last think, "I'm peckish. I know, I'll eat a cucumber"? But if you peel the cucumber, cut it into bite-sized morsels, then sprinkle it with a little salt, it becomes a delectable appetizer/between-meals nibble. Same with tomatoes: just cut them open, sprinkle a little salt (celery salt is especially good here) on the cut surface and enjoy. Lettuce hearts, broccoli stems, celery hearts—they are all equally delicious when served thus.

Sour fruit gets the same treatment: fresh sour cherries (*visne* in Turkish, or *albaloo* in Farsi) are hugely popular. They are washed and sprinkled with salt, or rolled in salt and then sun-dried and stored for a year-round treat. The cornelian cherry (*zogal akhteh* in Farsi), a variety of dogberry, is enjoyed the same way. Sour plums, which in the West we are told to avoid for fear of an upset tummy, are regarded as a favorite springtime delicacy: they are sold in the streets in Turkey, Iran, and the other -istans with a twist of salt on the side.

Fresh nuts are also popular street/snack fare: cob and hazelnuts still with their frilly skirts on, soft-skinned pistachios straight from the tree, still-green walnuts—these are all devoured with glee as their seasons arrive. I'll never forget the first time my best beloved washed a still-green, still-furry, practically-still-twitching almond (known as *chaghaleh badam* in Iran), dipped it in salt and ate it: I felt sure a trip to the emergency dentist would be in the cards. They are in fact a great treat and Jamshid and his brothers, all old enough to know better, frequently squabble over the last one.

The idea is that you soak them in water for a few hours, rub excess fur from the skin, then dip them in salt and crunch them. It's hard to describe the flavor: they taste, well, green—green and fresh. If you could bottle the essence of spring and drink it, it would taste like fresh green almonds.

All of which goes to prove that a little well-placed salt is OK, and that we do over-complicate stuff in the West.

LEMON-ROASTED ALMONDS WITH SAFFRON

This is one of our most popular imported products in our store: the salty citrusy flavor is impossible to resist. In case you can't make it to Peckham to buy them from us, here's everything you'll need to re-create the scrumdiddlyumptiousness of them in your own home.

MAKES A BOWLFUL
(WHETHER YOU SHARE
OR NOT IS UP TO YOU)
⅔ cup/150ml lemon juice (fresh
   is best, but you can cheat and use
   good bottled stuff)

½ tsp ground saffron steeped in
   ⅔ cup/150ml boiling water
1⅓ cups/7oz/200g raw almonds
3 tbsp olive oil
1½ tsp sea salt
1 tsp citric acid (aka lemon salt)

Mix the lemon juice and saffron water together. Spread the almonds out in a shallow dish, and trickle the juice-water over them, turning the nuts over in the liquid so that they are well coated. Leave them for around an hour, turning them occasionally.

After the time is up, drain the almonds and pat dry: unless you are at least a *rial* millionaire, I insist that you retain the saffron marinade in the name of thrift.*

Preheat the oven to 350°F/180°C.** Spread the almonds out on a small baking tray and bake them for around 10 minutes.

Next mix the oil and salts together in a bowl then tip in the hot almonds, stirring with a spoon to ensure that the nuts are all coated. Spread them back onto the baking tray and bake for a further 10–15 minutes, or until they are a rich golden brown.

Leave to cool a little before sampling: these dudes get really hot in the oven. I speak from burned-tongue experience. They will keep for 2–3 days: after that, they start to go a little soft, so best just to eat them all up real quick.

* Tip

Keep it in a little jar in the fridge. You can add it to fish, vegetables, salad dressings, roast chicken… Or just use it for more nuts.

** Note

As a serious food writer (ahem), I am undoubtedly supposed to be writing about the proper way to do stuff, but look: between you and I, these work out just as well in the microwave. Instead of cooking them for 10 minutes followed by a further 10–15, just cook them for 3 minutes followed by another 5 minutes. Obviously all microwaves vary, so do check that they are "roasted" to your satisfaction. They will seem soft at first, but crisp up as they cool.

ZA'ATAR-FRIED CHICKPEAS

First, a story about chickpeas from our friend, Mullah Nasruddin.

The wise Mullah was living a frugal existence, subsisting mostly on chickpeas and bread. His neighbor, who was a vizier to the King no less, lived on fine repasts provided by the royal palace. Puzzled by Nasruddin's contentment, he told his neighbor one day, "Nasruddin, if you too endeavored to ingratiate yourself at court, then you would not have to live on such peasant fare."

To which the Mullah replied, "But, my dear neighbor, if you too learned to live on chickpeas and bread, then you would not have to spend your time bowing and scraping in such obsequious fashion."

Chickpeas are really versatile: a great snack in their own right, they can also be used as croûtons in soup or salads, and they make for a pretty garnish for *houmous* (see p.120) and similar dips. They may seem humble fare, but they are full of tryptophan, which makes you happy: you should always listen to Nasruddin.

MAKES A BIG BOWLFUL

generous 1 cup/7oz/200g dried chickpeas, soaked for 6 hours or overnight

splodge of olive oil
1 tbsp sea salt
1 tbsp *za'atar**

Rinse and drain the chickpeas, then leave them until they are quite dry.

Heat a little oil in a frying pan and add the chickpeas, followed a minute or so later by the salt and spice. Cook, stirring constantly, for around 3 minutes before spooning out on to some paper towel to drain. Once again, leave them to cool a little before digging in. They will keep for a week or so in an airtight plastic tub—if you can leave them alone that long.

* A note on za'atar

Travelers who have previously visited Veggiestan (i.e. my last book) will know that *za'atar* is the Arabic word for thyme, and also a ubiquitous Arabic spice mixture comprising ground thyme, sumac, salt, and sesame. It is the latter that you need here.

Maghrebi Habas Fritas
SPICED ROASTED FAVA BEANS

Anyone who has tarried a while in a Spanish tapas bar will be familiar with *habas fritas*: fried (or roasted) split fava beans. Totally addictive, but not very good for those with crowns or implants.

In this recipe we see your *habas fritas* and raise them some very nice Moroccan spices to create the perfect nibble to have with a few drinks.

Drain and rinse the fava beans, then leave them to drain thoroughly.

Mix the olive oil with the spices and salt, then roll the hopefully-almost-dry beans in the oil, stirring well to ensure that they are all coated.

Preheat the oven to 340°F/170°C. Spread the beans out on a baking tray and bake them for around 30 minutes, or until they are crispy and golden brown. Leave to cool before sampling/sharing. These will keep a few days in an airtight container.

MAKES A BIG
BOWLFUL
generous 1 cup/7oz/200g dried,
    split fava (broad) beans,
    soaked for at least 6 hours
3 tbsp olive oil
1 tsp smoked paprika
½ tsp ground cumin
½ tsp ground ginger
½ tsp chili powder
1 tbsp garlic salt

DRY-ROASTED GREEN PEAS WITH FENUGREEK

This is another very addictive and almost healthy way to enjoy a modicum of salt. You can use fresh or frozen peas for this.

Rinse the peas and leave to drain (or roll them on paper towel to dry). Mix the oil with the spices and salt in a bowl, then tip in the peas, stirring gently (so as not to mash it all up) to ensure that the peas are all coated.

Preheat the oven to 300°F/150°C. Spread the spiced peas out on a baking tray (one with edges) and put them in the oven. After 15 minutes, turn the heat right down to 250°F/120°C, and allow your peas to cook for a further 45 minutes, turning them gently halfway through. Take the peas out of the oven and test one: it should be crunchy without breaking your teeth. These spicy peas will keep for a week in an airtight plastic tub.

MAKES A BOWLFUL
scant 2⅔ cups/10½ oz/300g
    common or garden peas
    (defrosted if necessary)
3 tbsp olive oil
1 level tbsp ground fenugreek
    seeds
1 tbsp cracked coriander seeds
1 tsp cayenne pepper
1 tsp paprika
1 tbsp celery salt (or sea salt)

SNACKISTANI SPICED VEGETABLE CHIPS

In an "ideal" world peopled by shiny Suzy Homemakers, every house would have a little tub of these almost healthy root vegetable chips ready for their hungry brood. This kind of snack exudes homeyness and wholesomeness. But don't let that put you off.

Vegetable chips are really easy to make and are useful in lunchboxes and on the *mezze* table alike. The addition of some Middle Eastern-style spices just takes them to the next level. We might actually have to patent them...

In each case the quantities should give you enough for one big bowlful.

CARROTS WITH CARDAMOM AND CUMIN

Carrots, cumin, and cardamom are a cozy threesome, oft found together on the pages of recipe books. It's a relationship that clearly works, so who am I to argue?

3 large carrots	½ tsp coarse ground black pepper
1½ tsp ground cardamom	½ tsp ground sea salt
1 tsp ground cumin	2 tbsp sunflower or canola oil

Preheat the oven to 375°F/190°C.

Peel the carrots and slice them very thinly. A mandoline would be handy here, although I find them scary and dangerous. The dextrous among you may well be able to shave off decent slices with a vegetable peeler.

Mix the spices and seasoning together with the oil, then toss the carrots in the mixture, turning them over until they are all coated. Spread them out on a baking tray and bake for 6–7 minutes, or until they are starting to brown and curl at the edges.

Cool them on a wire rack—they will crisp up more as they cool. These are pretty addictive on their own, but also team well with *houmous* (see p.120). They keep for a few days in a plastic tub.

BEETS WITH GINGER AND GARAM MASALA

Beets and ginger go together like Aladdin and his lamp. They just do. The addition of garam masala into the equation gives these chips an exotic extra something. Personally I eat these as fast as I can make them, but should you manage to retain some, they are perfect paired with tsatsiki. They also make a fancy accompaniment to fish or game dishes.

2 large beets	½ tsp salt
1 level tsp ground ginger	½ tsp ground black pepper
1 tsp garam masala	2 tbsp olive oil

Preheat the oven to 350°F/180°C.

Peel the beets and slice them as thinly as possible. Mix the spices and seasoning with the oil in a bowl, and add the beets, turning them until coated all over.

Spread the slices out on a baking tray (or two): it doesn't matter if they overlap a bit as they curl during the cooking process anyway. Cook for around 30 minutes, turning the tray around halfway through. Tip on to paper towel and leave to cool—they will crisp up once they are out of the oven. They should keep for a few days in an airtight container.

TURNIP WITH *DUKKAH*

Turnips aren't widely seen in chip form. This may be because they stay very slightly chewy—but to my mind this just makes them even more addictive.

3 medium turnips
1½ tbsp olive oil
1 good tbsp *dukkah**

* Dukkah: an Egyptian condiment
To make your own, lightly roast 1 tablespoon shelled hazelnuts (or almonds), 1 tablespoon sesame seeds, ½ tablespoon cumin seeds, and ½ tablespoon coriander seeds, and then grind them together with some salt and pepper to taste. This will keep for 2–3 weeks in a sealed container.

Preheat the oven to 350°F/180°C.

Peel the turnips and slice them thinly with a mandoline or sharp knife. Drizzle over the oil and turn the slices over with your hands to make sure they are coated. Spread them out on a baking tray and bake for 15 minutes. At this stage, sprinkle them with the *dukkah* on both sides, then put them back in the oven for a further 20 minutes, or until they start to turn a pleasant shade of golden brown.

Leave to cool on a wire rack. These are fine on their own, but also work well with dips or topped with smoked meat/cheeses. Eat within a day or so.

HARISSA POPCORN

An irresistible TV snack craftily designed to distract your friends/other half so you can grab the remote control...

MAKES A BIG BOWLFUL
3½ oz/100g unpopped popcorn
2 tbsp olive oil
2 tbsp Snackistan Patent Harissa Spice Mix
    (see below)

Pop the popping corn in a pan with a lid or in the microwave. Once it has stopped hissing and spitting, tip it into a bowl. Mix the olive oil with the spice mix and drizzle it over the popcorn, tossing it all together to ensure everything gets coated. Share around...

THE SNACKISTAN PATENT HARISSA SPICE MIX

This is a very secret recipe, so don't share it with anyone, alright? You can actually buy similar products in stores now, but it is more satisfying to make your own. Once you have used this spice mix, it is hard to imagine cooking without it. I have not yet managed to incorporate it into salted caramel, but give me time...

FILLS A 12OZ/300G JAR
2 tbsp coriander seeds
2 tbsp green cumin seeds
1 tbsp caraway seeds

1 tbsp red pepper flakes
1½ tsp garlic salt (garlic sea salt is better)
1 level tsp smoked paprika
1 tbsp dried mint

Toast (dry-fry) the first seeds in a frying pan, stirring constantly: they only need a couple of minutes. Set aside to cool a little.

After five minutes or so, toss the toasted spices with all the other ingredients, then whizz the mixture briefly in a coffee grinder in batches, or pound with a mortar and pestle. You don't want it to end up totally homogenized and powdered: some texture is desirable.

Store it in an airtight jar until you need it. Which I assure you will be quite often. Use on fish, chicken, salads, bread, pizza, lamb, vegetables, popcorn...

Tokhmeh Shor

ROASTED AND SALTED SEEDS

A wasteful bunch, us Westerners, when it comes to food by-products; if the usage thereof is complicated or time-consuming, we just toss 'em. Meat and fish bones, fruit and veggie peel, stale bread, limp salad produce: they all get jettisoned, mostly because we are simply too busy to think about using them—but also because we have collectively forgotten the virtues of culinary thrift.

Across Snackistan these things are all recycled into new and interesting foods: soups and stocks, fruit pastes and conserves, pickles and snacks galore. There is no better illustration of this than the use of seeds. Most members of the *Cucurbitaceae* family (that's melons and squash to you) have edible and super-nutritious seeds. Across South America, Africa, and the Middle East, these are used extensively in cooking and also roasted and salted and pressed into service as snack fodder. It does, admittedly, take a degree of lingual deftness in order to crack the things open and extract the kernel (although annoyingly parrots and those who are born in seed-eating countries seem to be able to eat five hundred a minute)—but most of them can, at a pinch, be crunched whole. And there is an almost Zen-like pleasure in working through a little bowl of them. They are so easy to make at home, and you get extra Brownie thrift points for so doing.

If you grow sunflowers it is easy to dry the seeds once the flowers are "over." Other seeds that routinely enter the Western kitchen are pumpkin, melon, watermelon, acorn squash, and butternut squash. To render them snackable, the healthy way is to wash them, then soak them in heavily salted water for a few hours. Next drain and spread them out on a baking tray then bake them at 350°F/180°C for around 30 minutes, or until golden brown.

For slightly naughtier seeds try the following:

Toss the washed and drained seeds in olive oil mixed with red pepper flakes, smoked paprika, and ground cumin (or use the Snackistan harissa mix, p.21) and roast as above for around 25 minutes.

Mix ground turmeric, curry powder, and citric acid (aka lemon salt) together with olive oil and again toss the seeds to coat thoroughly before baking as above.

Melt a little butter and mix it with olive oil: add 1 teaspoon ground cinnamon, ½ teaspoon ground cardamom, ½ teaspoon ground ginger, and 2 teaspoons brown sugar, and once again coat and bake the seeds for a lovely fragrant sweet version.

Zeitoun
OLIVES, MARINATED FOUR WAYS

A bowl of olives is perhaps the simplest *mezze* item of all. The strong flavors challenge the taste buds in a way that few other foods do, while for those of us who live in climes less warm, to bite into a flavored olive is to sup of Flora and the country green: one is immediately, briefly, deliciously transported to, well, somewhere that isn't one's local main street or bar and grill. Olives may be small and low in calories, but the sensual ritual of eating them can leave one feeling quite replete. There again, for the (guesstimated) 33 percent of the population who actually loathe olives, they are of course the snack from Hades.

Most self-respecting delicatessen counters are heaving with already-marinated olives, but it is so much more fun to create your own. Here are four slightly different ways to prepare them at home.

for Green Olives

Rinse and drain around 1lb 2oz/500g green olives in brine. Cut a small cross in the bottom of each (fiddly but worth it), then add one of the following marinades and leave overnight:

Mix around 2 tablespoons of extra-virgin olive oil with 1 teaspoon rosemary, 1 teaspoon dried savory (or thyme), 3 crushed juniper berries, and a measure of raki (or ouzo, or pastis). Good with a glass of wine.

Toast (dry-fry) 1 teaspoon fenugreek seeds with 2 teaspoons mustard seeds until they pop. Crush the seeds with a mortar and pestle, then add ½ teaspoon asafoetida* (optional: or you can use ½ a grated onion and 1 minced garlic clove instead), and 2 tablespoons olive oil. Pairs well with *doogh* or *ayran* (aka salted yogurt drink).

for Black Olives

Rinse and drain 1lb 2oz/500g Kalamata-style black olives in brine. Chop/mash 2 garlic cloves, around 6 anchovies, 6 sun-dried tomatoes, and 1 tablespoon capers together, then add 1 tablespoon red wine vinegar and 1 tablespoon olive oil to the mixture. Stir through the olives, chill, and leave for a few hours. This is great on *mezze* spreads, or in salads/on pizzas. Nice with a fancy aperitif.

Buy 1lb 2oz/500g salted Moroccan or Turkish-style olives (they're the oily, wrinkly ones). Crush 1 teaspoon rose petals together with 2 teaspoons Snackistan harissa spice mix (p.21), then add 1 teaspoon red pepper flakes and 1 tablespoon olive oil. Drizzle over the olives and mix well. Leave for a few hours before enjoying with a cold beer.

A note on asafoetida

Ah. Asafoetida. Don't be put off by the smell. It is famously used in Indian cuisine as a substitute for garlic and onion, which certain castes are prohibited from eating. It is also used in the kitchens of the Eastern and South Eastern extremities of Snackistan: Arabia, Afghanistan, and Pakistan. It is collected as a resin, which can be ground into a powder or used whole (in which case, it needs to be exposed to heat to do any good). Whatever you do with it, the most important thing to remember about it is that a little goes a long way.

It is perhaps most interesting when used as a remedy. Traveler Charles Doughty noted in his book *Travels in Arabia Deserta* that it is a "drug which the Arabs have in sovereign estimation." It has a slightly anesthetizing effect, and thus can be used for toothache and sore throats, but it is also (reputedly) good at treating flatulence, viral complaints, headaches, stress, and menstrual pain. Boil a little resin (if possible) or a teaspoon of powder in a cupful of water and sip at it slowly, pinching your nose to escape the "aroma."

fishy Things

Fish cuisine in the Middle East is largely limited to the areas that have access to, well, water. It is sad that in the Middle West we can effectively buy anything anytime anywhere. Snackistan remains far more in touch with its culinary heritage and this invariably entails eating locally-sourced, seasonal produce.

I asked one of my regular Afghan customers whether he had eaten much fish back home: Afghanistan is after all a landlocked country. He replied that since his village is next to a large lake, whenever his mother wanted to cook fish she would send one of her boys out to catch some. When I asked him which fish he caught, he just smiled and said the Pashto equivalent of "Whatever!"

That does not mean that material for this chapter was limited: quite the opposite, as the region comprises the Caspian, the Persian Gulf, the Mediterranean, and the Black Sea as well as any number of freshwater resources. Fishing references there are aplenty in the Bible, and our friend Nasruddin himself is often to be found out in a fishing boat…

The Mullah and his neighbor went fishing one day and took a boat out from the pool in the harbor. They fished and they fished and eventually the boat was full of mullet and bream.

"Be sure to mark this spot so we can come back tomorrow," cried the happy Mullah to his friend. "At this rate we will have enough to sell at market."

The next day they returned to the dock in eager anticipation.

"I hope you marked our fishing ground clearly," said Nasruddin.

"I certainly did," said his neighbor, "I put a big black cross on the bottom of the dinghy."

"You idiot!" exclaimed the Mullah in frustration, "What if we can't find the same boat to use today?"

WARM BARBERRY AND FANCY SHRIMP WITH LENTILS

MEZZE DISH FOR 8
OR APPETIZER FOR 4

1¼ cups/9oz/250g Puy lentils
3½ oz/100g barberries*
big pat of butter and dash of oil
around 16 really meaty jumbo
    shrimp, peeled and deveined
⅓ tsp ground saffron steeped
    in a splosh of boiling water
4 tbsp olive oil
½ in/1cm fresh ginger, minced
3 tbsp pomegranate molasses**
juice and zest of 1 lime
salt and coarsely ground
    black pepper
4 scallions, chopped
½ bunch each of fresh mint
    and parsley, stemmed
    and chopped

* Barberries

If you can't find barberries
(try your local Middle Eastern
store), then substitute with
cranberries in the winter, and
redcurrants in the summer.

** Pomegranate molasses

There are now, amazingly, quite
a few varieties of pomegranate
molasses from which to choose,
such is the trendiness of this
ingredient in the West. In this
context, an Arabic one is a
better bet: it is less dark and
gloopy and a little less sour.

This is one with real wow factor. Although, you show most people a plate of shrimp and they get excited regardless of how you prepare them. I never cease to marvel at the popularity of all things shrimp-like.

There are quite a few traditional Middle Eastern shrimp recipes, mostly from the area around the Gulf and the Mediterranean littoral. But Muslims in some parts of Snackistan avoid them altogether, owing to a continuing debate as to whether they are halal (some fish is, but each sect/mullah interprets the issue differently): many regard them as *makrouh*, which means they're frowned upon but not disallowed.

A more authentic *mezze* dish might be simply prepared shrimp cooked with butter, lemon, and parsley—but this one will elicit far more oohs and aahs, and even the odd *mash'Allah* (a generic Arabic term of appreciation with religious overtones—literally: "God has willed it").

Pick through the lentils (even big brands can still contain small stones) and place them in a pan of cold water. Bring to a boil and cook for around 30 minutes, or until they are just cooked. Drain and leave to cool.

Next check through the barberries, which can also contain half the countryside, and soak them in cold water for around 20 minutes. This will enable any residual sediment/barbs to sink to the bottom of the bowl. After this time, carefully scoop the berries out of the water, squeezing the moisture out.

Melt the butter in a frying pan along with a splash of oil (to stop the butter burning) and lower in the shrimp. Sauté for around 3 minutes before adding the barberries (unless you are using cooked shrimp, in which case you can cook the berries and shrimp at the same time), then cook for 2 minutes more, stirring constantly. Next, add the saffron water, mix well, and take off the heat.

Whisk the 4 tablespoons oil, ginger, pomegranate molasses, lime juice and zest, and seasoning together in a bowl.

Finally, mix it all together. Stir the shrimp and barberries through the lentils, drizzle with the dressing, then finally, stir in the onions and herbs. Serve while it is all still warm.

GULF-STYLE SWORDFISH CEVICHE

MEZZE FOR 6–8

1 small papaya*

1lb 2oz/500g swordfish, skinned
and cut into ½ in/1.5cm cubes

1 large red onion, finely diced

1 small red bell pepper, finely
diced

½ Scotch bonnet or Habanero,
or 2–3 green chilies, minced

2 garlic cloves, minced

3 limes and 3 sour oranges** (or
5 limes and 1 regular orange)

⅓ tsp ground saffron steeped in
a dash of boiling water

½ tsp freshly ground
black pepper

1 tsp sea salt

½ bunch each of fresh cilantro
and mint, chopped

TO SERVE:

nice lettuce (Romaine is good)

Snackistan nachos

* A note on papaya
I realize that papaya may not be
readily available everywhere, so
do feel free to substitute kiwi—it
has a similar softening effect on
meat and fish.

** Sour oranges
aka Seville oranges
These grow across much of
Snackistan, and both the dried
peel and the juice are used
extensively in Persian and Turkish
food. If you can't find them, just
substitute a little regular orange
mixed with extra lemon or lime.

Shopkeepers don't travel very much: they don't need to. If you run a store on a main street in Anytown, Anystan, eventually the world will come to you. Um, there is also the thing that it is hard getting people to run your store for you while you're away, but we don't dwell on that.

Anyway, the upshot of this is that when we do go away, we tend to get over-excited. So a recent brief trip to the United Arab Emirates had me dancing around like a kiddie in a candy bazaar, not least at the prospect of trying Gulf food.

So very international is the region now that it is quite hard to find truly authentic Emirati cuisine: it is strongly influenced by migrants from India, Persia, and Europe, and most restaurants attempt to cover all bases by offering a "buffet." Once the traveler gets over the disappointment of being offered a range of miscellaneous things in chafing dishes, this is a good way to sample a huge number of foodstuffs, for what is a buffet but a self-serve *mezze* table? Thus, serendipitously, I rediscovered ceviche, a dish I hadn't made for years. In this case, it was made with hammour (grouper), which is the Gulf's most widely consumed food fish: I have substituted swordfish, which is often more readily available—but you could also use sea bass, salmon, or tuna. It works well as a *mezze* dish, appetizer, or a light summer snack. Papaya is not indigenous to the region (which is, let's face it, mostly desert), but has been found to grow well there.

Peel the papaya and scoop out the seeds, retaining six of them. Chop the flesh into ½in/1.5cm cubes. Place the fish and fruit in a plastic tub (one that has a lid, preferably), or a plastic bag, together with the onion, peppers, chilies, and garlic.

Zest about half of the citrus fruit and extract the juice from all of it. Crush the reserved papaya seeds. Mix the zest and juice with the saffron, pepper, salt, papaya seeds, and herbs and tip it over the swordfish, mixing well. Cover and chill for 6–12 hours, stirring halfway through.

Serve with lettuce leaves (great for wrapping around the ceviche) and spiced nachos.

BONUS RECIPE: NACHOS!

Gather up all your stale flatbread and spread it out on a baking sheet. Preheat the oven to 400°F/200°C. Mix a little olive oil with *za'atar* or the Snackistan Patent Harissa Spice Mix (see p.21) and some salt, and brush each of the bread pieces with the mixture. Bake the "nachos" for around 10 minutes, or until they are golden brown. Don't let them overcook as they will harden when they come out of the oven. Keep in a covered plastic tub for a few days: perfect snack fodder and great with dips and ceviche.

CANDLES INN TARAMOSALATA

**MAKES A BIG
BOWLFUL**

5–6 slices of stale white bread,
    crusts removed

2 tbsp *tarama* paste (about
    3oz/80g), or 2 smoked fish
    roes (about 5½ oz/150g)

1 medium onion, cut into chunks

juice of 2 small lemons

¾–1¼ cups/ 200–280ml corn
    oil (olive oil can be used but
    is really far too heavy for
    this dish)

Taramosalata: smoked fish roe dip, a lynchpin of Greek and Turkish menus in practically any taverna or *meyhane* anywhere in the world. And a strong contender for the title of the world's most fattening dish. Not that I want to put you off or anything. The trouble with taramosalata is that it is quite addictive: one of those foods that you just keep scarfing until you've had far too much.

I made so much of it during the years I spent working in Greek restaurants (including the Candles Inn of the title) that I used to dream in pink. Except of course real cod roe is not that brightly colored and many chefs resort to food coloring to lend the dish its trademark "chichi-ness."

It is easy to make at home—if you have a blender (no worries if you don't—it will just take you longer). It is an emulsion, and so, like mayonnaise, relies on the gentle addition of oil to other ingredients.* The trickiest part of the whole operation is finding the smoked fish roe. In Greece, carp or mullet roe is used, but the most common by far is cod. The good news is that all good fishmongers sell "fresh smoked" cods' roe, and *tarama* paste (salted roe) is available in most Greek and Turkish stores. Note that the fresh roe does not have quite such a strong flavor as the paste and so you will need to use a little more.

Soak the bread in cold water for 10 minutes or so.

Put half of the *tarama* in a blender along with half of the onion and give it a quick whizz. Squeeze the water out of the bread and add half of it to the pink purée along with half of the lemon juice. Blend it for a good few minutes—you need the bread to be broken up and the paste to be distributed evenly.

Trickle the oil in very very slowly while the machine is running. Keep going until the mixture is thick, glossy, and smooth and will absorb no more oil—the quantity of oil will vary slightly according to how big your lemons were and how much moisture was left in the bread, but it should be about ½ cup/125ml. Scoop the first batch out and repeat with the other half of the ingredients. If it curdles, don't despair: just empty the blender (retaining the contents), wash it, and run it under cold water to cool it, then start a new batch using the curdled gunk in place of oil. It will be fine, promise.

Serve chilled: finely chopped dill or parsley and an olive are the traditional garnishes. Hot pita bread is a requisite.

*

A note on emulsifying

My father was a paint chemist, and I spent many a happy hour watching him mix paints in his workshop. Nothing proved more satisfying than watching stuff emulsify, and the same principle is true in the kitchen. I still do a little happy dance every time I manage to make a batch of mayonnaise without it curdling. Don't tell anyone, ok?

RENA SALAMAN'S SHRIMP *YIOUVETSI*

Books about Greek food are myriad, but I only own one. (Actually, it's not even mine, but rather my mother's: I really should give it back to her one day, but I've had it for nearly 30 years so maybe she's forgotten, eh?)

When I worked in assorted Greek restaurants, Rena Salaman's *Greek Food* was my constant companion. Her anecdotal and highly informative style of writing truly transports the reader to the window of the *taverna* kitchen, and the recipes are as authentic as you will find anywhere.

The dish of *yiouvetsi* gets its name from the brown earthenware dish in which it is cooked: lamb and chicken *yiouvetsi* are also common. This is a lovely, summery, light *mezze* dish: very Mediterranean. Ms. Salaman writes of supping on *yarithes yiouvetsi* while overlooking "sleepy interlocking emerald bays bordered by white luminous sandy beaches and dense pine trees reflected in the still waters." Don't fret: I'm sure your dining room will be just as evocative. This is her recipe, with slightly increased quantities...

Preheat the oven to 350°F/180°C.

Blanch the shrimp in just a little boiling water for around 3 minutes before draining them and reserving the cooking liquid. Set the shrimp aside while you make the sauce.

Fry the onion and garlic in the olive oil, then add the herbs, wine, tomatoes, and a few tablespoons of the shrimp cooking stock. Season to taste and simmer gently for a couple of minutes.

When the shrimp are just cool enough to handle, peel all but four of them. Next, devein them if needed: if they have a black streak down the back, just pull it away with a sharp knife (the black vein is their "wastage system" and is best not eaten). The four reserved shrimp should be shelled and deveined, but leave the heads and tails intact.

Arrange the shrimp in one large or four small *yiouvetsi* (oven dishes), propping the ones with the heads still on against the side of the dish so it looks as if they are peeking over the edge (just for fun). Pour the sauce over the seafood, sprinkle it liberally with parsley, and spread the feta over the top. Bake for around 20 minutes.

Enjoy with warm bread, and maybe dig out that old *bouzouki* CD you brought back from your vacation.

MEZZE FOR 8
OR APPETIZER FOR 4
OR SUPPER FOR 2

1lb 2oz/500g shell-on raw jumbo shrimp—you can use cooked, peeled ones if you are in a hurry

1 large onion, finely sliced

2 garlic cloves, minced (my addition)

½ cup/120ml olive oil

2 tsp dried oregano or thyme

about ⅔ cup/150ml white wine

1lb 2oz/500g fresh tomatoes, skinned and sliced (or use equivalent canned)

salt and freshly ground black pepper

big handful of chopped parsley

7oz/200g feta, thinly sliced

STREETWISE SARDINES

MEZZE FOR 6

6 large fresh whole sardines,
    scaled and gutted

olive oil

salt and freshly ground
    black pepper

3 tbsp *chermoula* (optional:
    see bonus recipe below)

6–12 grape leaves,
    depending on size

lemon wedges

The sardine is another critter perfectly designed for snacking. It's easy to pull apart, highly nutritious, and when it's cooked properly, so very tasty. Therein lies the rub: there are so many badly cooked sardines being dished up all over the world that it is quite off-putting. The chief problem is that they are usually over-cooked or cooked from frozen, which leads them to disintegrate rather swiftly. I have also been served sardines that are burned on the outside and raw in the middle, and those that have been improperly cleaned and not exactly fresh. The trouble is that once you have eaten something that is perfectly prepared, it is hard to accept second best: anyone who has eaten smoky, freshly grilled, lemon-squeezed sardines with their fingers while strolling the chattering evening streets of anywhere warm-by-the-sea will understand what I mean.

The secret is to use very fresh fish. Frozen are just about acceptable if you defrost them properly. The other Snackistani secret is to wrap them in vine leaves: this stops them from burning, helps the fish remain moist, and makes them easier to deal with should you wish to do that warm-by-the-sea thing and eat it with your fingers while walking around the backyard.

They are lovely grilled without any extra flavoring, but I offer you the *chermoula* option for when you are cooking for persnickety "oh it smells/tastes fishy" types.

Drizzle the sardines with olive oil inside and out, and gently rub in some salt and pepper. If using *chermoula*, fill the cavity with the rub and marinate at room temperature for around 30 minutes before cooking.

If you are using fresh vine leaves, blanch them for 2–3 minutes before using: if you are using preserved vine leaves, give them a quick rinse before use as they are very salty. Wrap each fish in one big or two small leaves (the head and tail do not need to be covered), and brush the outside of each leaf with a little olive oil.

Preheat your barbecue or grill and cook the fish for around 3 minutes on each side. (Alternatively, you can bake these in an oven preheated to 400°F/200°C for around 20 minutes.) The traditional thing of a fish being cooked when its eyes whiten holds true with sardines.

Serve with chunky bread (best for fish—it acts as an emergency aid should someone splutter on a bone) and lemon wedges, together with any surplus *chermoula* sauce.

BONUS RECIPE: *CHERMOULA*

Chermoula is a classic Moroccan sauce, although confusingly it has appeared on the market recently as a dry spice mix. It goes with just about any savory dish, especially fish, and is easy to whizz together. Just blend or pound together half a bunch of fresh cilantro, 1 tablespoon paprika, 1 teaspoon red pepper flakes, 1½ teaspoons ground cumin, 3 garlic cloves, ¼ teaspoon ground saffron, grated zest and juice of ½ a lemon, and 2½ tablespoons olive oil. Use as a marinade, rub, or to drizzle on stuff. Will keep for a week in the fridge.

ANCHOVY LOLLIPOPS (*BANDERILLAS*)

Now I think snacks on cocktails sticks are due for a comeback. After all, Black Forest cake, jumpsuits, lava lamps, and cupcakes have all discovered renewed trendiness. Cheese and pineapple can't be far behind...

These little numbers are based on the Spanish *tapas* idea of *banderillas* (named after matadors' stabby things), but have an extra Middle Eastern twist. They are so simple I feel slightly embarrassed presenting this as a recipe: it is more a serving suggestion than anything else.

While I am sure you have better things to do with your day than scour hardware stores measuring their cocktail sticks, it is worth trying to source slightly longer ones for this recipe.

MAKES AROUND 12

12 quails' eggs

2 tsp *za'atar*

12 baby Turkish-style pickled chilies

14 nice pitted olives (garlic stuffed would be cool)

6 Iranian pickled cucumbers (you could use the ones you made on p.12), halved horizontally

12 plump anchovies (the ones in vinegar work best here as they are firmer)

handful of large cilantro, parsley, basil, and mint leaves

Boil the quails' eggs for around 4 minutes before peeling and halving them. Once they are cool, rub the cut face of each half in a little *za'atar* and sandwich them back together.

Thread all the ingredients, interspersed with bits of herb, onto 12 cocktail sticks. The anchovy should be folded accordion-style. And that's it: a great little munch, offering soft, crispy, salt, sour, spicy, umami, and plenty of color.

Psaria

GREEK-STYLE FRIED FISH WITH VINEGAR SAUCE

Seminal seafood meals are invariably rendered thus by the experience of sitting by the sea, watching the sun play on the water, maybe dangling a toe in the briny deep and patently not being at work. But the good news for those of us trying to recapture that whole thing at home is that the other secret of great seafood is that "less is more." The best fish I have ever eaten has been the most simply prepared, and nowhere do they understand this better than in Greece.

The most popular and common way to cook fish is to flour and then fry it: this serves the dual purpose of locking the flavor and aroma in, thus reducing lingering fish smells. The beauty of the Greek and Cypriot approach is that it is not dependent on the type of fish: they will buy a bag of assorted fish and cook it all the same way. Chat to your fishmonger and ask which fish he recommends for frying: you want either small whole fish, or slightly larger ones that have been filleted: baby mullet, sardines, herrings, mackerel, and sprats are obvious choices.

The vinegar sauce is a traditional accompaniment and just adds a little bit of tongue-tickling oomph.

CLASSIC *MEZZE* FOR 4–6

1lb 12oz/800g cleaned, filleted (unless the fish are teeny), and scaled fish
salt
all-purpose flour (generous 1 cup/5½ oz/150g should be enough)
1 tsp paprika
1 tsp ground turmeric
sunflower or canola oil (corn oil is more authentic—but I find it a bit heavy)
3 garlic cloves
1 tsp fresh or dried rosemary
scant ½ cup/100ml white wine vinegar
big handful of fresh parsley, chopped
freshly ground black pepper

Wash the fish and dry with paper towel before sprinkling it with salt. Mix 3 tablespoons of flour with some more salt, along with the paprika and turmeric. Coat each piece of fish with the flour mixture and shake off any excess (sift and reserve any flour that is left over).

Next heat about ¼in/1.5cm of oil in a frying pan and fry the fish for around 2 minutes on each side, or until they are golden brown; once they are cooked, transfer them to an ovensafe dish.

Strain around 3 tablespoons of the cooking oil into a saucepan and bring it back to sizzle point. Toss in the garlic and rosemary, then add around 1½ tablespoons of flour (using the flour you collected above), stirring well so it forms a roux. Slowly add the vinegar, plus a little water if it still looks very thick, then add the parsley and season to taste.

Finally, pour the sauce over the fish. You can serve the fish as it is, but more traditionally the dish is left to cool for an hour or so and served at room temperature or chilled: this enables the flavors to mingle and get to know each other.

Oolonganch Litsk
ARMENIAN STUFFED MUSSELS

Much of the Muslim world regards shellfish (and any seafood without scales) as *haram* or taboo. As most of Snackistan is Muslim, this means that the consumption of mussels is not that widespread, but in Armenia and Turkey they are really popular as street food and *mezze* dishes.

I have to admit that I was a bit puzzled by the popularity and diversity of shellfish recipes in Armenia: it is, after all, landlocked and not particularly well stocked with freshwater species. But Armenia has shrunk over the millennia, and it previously boasted both a Caspian Sea littoral and easy access to the Black Sea and the Mediterranean. The Turks, of course, have a huge coastline and a long-standing love of seafood.

MEZZE FOR 6

18–24 large fresh mussels, cleaned
    and debearded
salt
scant ½ cup/2¾oz/75g currants
1 large onion, chopped
pat of butter
½ cup/2¾oz/75g pine nuts

1 tsp ground allspice
1 tsp dried dill
salt and freshly ground black pepper
½ cup/4½ oz/125g short-grain rice
big handful of fresh parsley, chopped
olive oil
juice of 1 lemon

Place the mussels in a bowl of lukewarm salted water and leave for 30 minutes, or so: this tricks them into opening (throw away any that don't open), whereupon you can disarm their closure mechanism, thus making you feel like a piscatorial James Bond. You should also soak the currants.

Next, fry the onion in a blob of melted butter: once it becomes translucent, add the pine nuts, spice, dill, and a little seasoning, followed by the rice. Take off the heat and stir the parsley through the mixture.

Now take each mussel in turn and, using a small knife, gently prize them open from the fat end towards the pointy bit: you are aiming to sever the ligament at the pointy end, but you want the shell halves to remain attached. Once done, wash the mussels again in cold water.

Spoon a little of the rice mixture (about 2 teaspoonsful) into each mussel, press the shell together, and arrange them carefully in a saucepan. Place a plate on top of the shellfish, then add a good splash of olive oil, together with the lemon juice and enough water to cover the mussels. Bring the contents of the pan to a boil, then turn down the heat and simmer for around 45 minutes. Take off the heat and serve the mussels with extra lemon wedges. I like these hot, but they are traditionally served at room temperature and may also be enjoyed chilled.

TUNISIAN TUNA *BRIK*

Brik is derived from the Turkish word *boregi*, but basically we are talking pie here. Fish pie.

This book would not have been written had things turned out differently on a package vacation to Tunisia when I was 13. Any of you got a 13-year-old daughter? Sheesh, they can be obnoxious at times. Anyway, as an effort to persuade me to behave, my father totally convinced me that he had been offered six camels to leave me in the *souk*. It worked.

While our hotel food on that trip was memorable for all the wrong reasons, the street food of Sousse and Tunis was astonishingly good. These little fish pies stood out in my memory for flavor, plus they contain a delightful surprise.

They are traditionally made with a special thin, elastic pastry called *oarka*: this is hard to find in the West, but spring roll wrappers (or filo pastry at a pinch) make a great alternative.

MAKES 4

1 large onion, chopped
sunflower oil, for frying
1 small can (7oz/200g) tuna (sustainable, of course), drained
½ cup/3½ oz/100g pitted green olives, chopped
1 tbsp capers

2 tbsp chopped fresh parsley
1 tbsp chopped fresh mint
freshly ground black pepper
4 sheets *brik* pastry (*oarka*) or 4 spring roll wrappers (egg roll skins)
4 smallish eggs, plus 1 beaten egg if using *brik* pastry

Fry the onion in a dash of oil until it softens, then take off the heat and stir in the tuna, olives, capers, herbs, and black pepper.

Stretch the pastry or spring roll wrappers out on a clean board. Put a quarter of the tuna mixture on one half of each sheet, making a well in the center of the mixture. Now crack an egg into each well before folding the other half of the pastry carefully over the tuna (to form a semicircle or triangle, depending on the pastry you're using). Crimp the edges of the pastry with wet fingers to seal each "parcel." If you are using *brik* sheets, which are bigger than spring roll wrappers, fold the crimp again and brush the edges with beaten egg, as they are otherwise reluctant to stick.

Heat about ½in/1cm of oil in a frying pan (or use a deep fryer) and once it is sizzling, lower in the *briks* very gently. Cook them for around 2 minutes before turning them over and frying the other side for a further minute.

Remove the pastries from the oil, drain on paper towel, and allow to cool a little before serving with plenty of lemon wedges. And napkins, because if you are lucky, the egg will still be runny. Oh, and perhaps a cup of nice mint tea.

Kebab-e-Mahi

CASPIAN FISH KEBABS

An observation. When you are trying to compel those whose regular diet rarely includes fish on a voluntary basis, sticking the stuff on sticks and making it look like chicken is a maneuver of great culinary cunning. And one to which I have stooped on several occasions.

Chunky sturgeon kebabs are a stalwart of restaurant menus all round the Caspian: the more northerly nations (Russia, Kazakhstan) prepare it with yogurt and pomegranate paste, whereas Iranians are more likely to marinate it in saffron, onion, and lemon juice (like the *Jujeh Kebab* recipe on p.50). What I have done here is to take a northern dish and give it a southern twist: this fenugreek and tamarind marinade is typical of the hot cities and ports of the Persian Gulf. And don't panic: if your fishmonger is all out of sturgeon, this recipe will work with any firm fish, such as monkfish tail, tuna, swordfish, conga eel, or halibut.

MEZZE FOR 8

1 tsp fenugreek seeds, coarsely ground
sunflower oil, for frying
1 tbsp chopped fenugreek leaves
    (dried or fresh)
1 good tsp tamarind paste
4 garlic cloves, minced
¾ in/2cm piece fresh ginger, peeled
    and minced

½ tsp salt
½ tsp red pepper flakes
14oz/400g fish, filleted, skinned, and cut
    into 1¼ in/3cm cubes

TO SERVE:
juice of ½ lemon
iceberg lettuce leaves

Fry the fenugreek seeds in a little oil for a few minutes before adding the fenugreek leaves; cook for a minute or so more, stirring regularly, then take off the heat. When the mixture has cooled a little, blend it with the tamarind, garlic, ginger, salt, and red pepper flakes, adding a little oil to make it workable, and rub the resulting paste all over the fish. Either throw the fish in a plastic bag and let it sit at room temperature for 30 minutes, or put it in the fridge to marinate for 2 hours.

When you are ready to serve, thread the fish cubes onto either presoaked wooden skewers (see p.47) or oiled metal ones and grill over hot charcoal (or under a preheated broiler) for around 6 minutes, turning once or twice (the fish, not you). It is quite fun to serve this with lemon-drizzled iceberg lettuce leaves: *mezze* munchers can then use a leaf to scoop up and wrap the fish, obviating the need for separate lemon wedges, silverware, and finger bowls. If you want to make a meal of it, these kebabs can be served over rice along with the Patent Snackistan Kebab Salad Mix on p.63.

ON CAVIAR

Sturgeon, as I am sure you know, is caviar's mommy. And caviar is of course one of Iran's most famous exports, not to mention one of the world's most expensive snacks. Back in the (pre-Islamic state) day, it was traditionally enjoyed with a vodka chaser, but in truth nowadays most Iranians don't rate it very highly. After a lot of pollution and over-fishing during the last 50 years, the industry is now (quite rightly) tightly controlled by the Iranian government. Caviar is only sold at official outlets in Iran, which is also a good move as tales of its potential for food poisoning are justified.

Here, it is available from good Persian stores, but it is always best to get a quote first; you also need to decide which grade you want—there is sevruga, astra, and beluga—they're all good, but there is a vast difference in price and it varies monthly.

OF GOG AND MAGOG

Fascinating place, the Caspian Sea—it hides more than oil and fancy fish eggs in its depths. Firstly, over the millennia its levels have risen and fallen in quite dramatic fashion, swallowing bits of the littoral, palaces, villages, all kinds of historical bric-a-brac. Archaeologists have begun piecemeal research into castles, such as the one at Sabayil (submerged just off the coast of Azerbaijan), but there is still great mystery surrounding its origins.

Even more mysterious are the legends concerning the mountains of the region. There are a vast number of tales of ferocious tribes to the north, and a huge gate or wall built in the mountains to keep them out. The mythical consensus has it that the tribes had something to do with Gog and Magog (who are mentioned in both the Koran and the Bible), although whether these were your actual run-of-the-mill giants, the names of the tribes, or in fact the names of mountains, we will probably never know. In Farsi, the Caspian is known as *Darya-ye-Khazar*—the sea of the Khazaria: these latter were actually a warrior tribe living north of the Caucasus, and they too have become associated with the Gog/Magog stories. They converted to Judaism in the seventh century, leading some to speculate that they comprised descendants of the Ten Lost Tribes of Israel.

The fabled wall or gate in the mountains (which is referred to as *Uberi Aquilonis*—the "Breasts of the North") is most likely to have been located at the Azeri city of Darband (which means "closed gate" in Farsi), and is rumored either to have been erected by Alexander the Great, or by Dhulkarnain, the warrior protector of Islam. It was made of a mysterious fire-resistant element, and topped with (depending on the bit of ancient hearsay to which you subscribe) brambles, a freaky shrieking eagle, or naturally occurring scary-sounding "trumpets" (these were eventually blocked when owls nested there: this was thought to be the reason that the barbarians eventually escaped). It was believed that Armageddon would surely follow when this magical forcefield was breached from the north…

Why am I telling you all of this? Well, for three reasons. Firstly, it will surely stand you in good stead at the next trivia night. Secondly, it is, quite simply, fascinating. And thirdly, to show you how random research can be—all I did was to look up fish species in the Caspian Sea.

Kibbeh Samak

LEBANESE FISH AND LEMON *KIBBEH* PIE

Kibbeh are the Rubik's cubes of the snack world: oval bulgar croquettes filled with a loose stuffing—fiendish things to make. Not this one, though. This is made as a rough pie, and is altogether a different kettle (well, baking tray) of fish.

SERVES 4

FOR THE SHELL:

1¼ cups/6oz/175g fine bulgar (cracked wheat)
1lb 2oz/500g white fish fillets, skinned
1 large onion, roughly chopped
about ⅓ bunch each of fresh cilantro
    and parsley
grated zest of 1 lime
½ tsp ground cumin
½ tsp ground cinnamon
¼ tsp baking soda
salt and freshly ground black pepper

FOR THE FILLING:

olive oil, for frying
4 medium onions, chopped
¾ cup/3½oz/100g pine nuts (or use the
    infinitely cheaper sunflower seed kernels)
about 14 anchovy fillets
1 tbsp capers
1 preserved lemon, chopped (or dice and seed
    half of that lime you zested for the shell)
¼ tsp ground saffron steeped in a splash of
    boiling water

Preheat the oven to 400°F/200°C.

Wash the bulgar in cold water (use a very fine sieve, or a regular one lined with strong paper towel). Leave to drain while you make the rest of the shell.

Pop all the other shell ingredients in a blender and whizz for 2 minutes (or chop them very finely by hand and mix them thoroughly together). Add the contents of the blender to the bulgar in a bowl, and knead well: you need it to form a smooth paste.

To make the filling, heat a splash of olive oil in a frying pan and cook the onions; as they start to brown, add the pine nuts (reserving a dozen for garnish), anchovies (again, keep a few back), capers, and lemon, followed a minute later by the saffron water. Take off the heat.

Next grease a round baking dish, about 11–12in/28–29cm in diameter, or an equivalent-sized rectangular one, with a little olive oil. Press half the bulgar mixture into the bottom of the dish, using the heel of your palm to push it down and ensure even distribution. Top this layer with the onion and pine nut mixture, then spread the remaining bulgar mixture on top. This is not as easy as it sounds: you can either make lots of little balls of the dough and gently spread them over the filling until they join up, or you can use my patent method, which is to press the dough into a wet plate of roughly the same size, and then transfer it swiftly to sit on top of the filling. Score through the pie diagonally to divide it into bite-sized portions: it is easier to do this now than when it is just out of the oven. Finally, dot the reserved pine nuts and stripe the spare anchovies across the top to make it look pretty. Drizzle some olive oil over the pie and bake for around 30 minutes, or until it is golden brown and sizzling.

Serve hot or warm with extra lemon wedges. Can also be enjoyed cold as picnic fare.

SQUIDDLY DIDDLY TWO WAYS

Squid—it's such a well-designed food. It's easy to clean, fun to cook, and perfect for snacking. It readily absorbs/goes with almost any flavor you throw at it. And it is full of protein, trace minerals (including selenium), and vitamin B.

You can buy frozen, pre-cleaned squid tubes from most supermarkets now, but fresh squid does have the edge on flavor and tenderness. If you are reading this with a slimy fresh squid in front of you wondering what to do, well... firstly, cut off the tentacles just above the lumpy bit between the eyes. Next, locate the weird "plastic" backbone inside the tube of the squid: edge your forefinger around it and grasp it between your thumb and said digit, wrapping the other fingers around the rest of the innards. You should now be able to pull the spine and all of that gooey squiddy doo-da stuff out. Finally, run some cold water into the tube to clean it, then rinse off the tentacles, and presto. Now at this stage you could just coat it in seasoned flour and fry it. Or you could try something a little different...

SQUID COOKED IN FIZZY ORANGE TAMARIND BATTER

Batter is great when made with sparkling stuff: beer, *doogh* (yogurt drink), carbonated water, or soda. The slight citrus flavor of the "orange" in this batter contrasts well with the tamarind, and they combine to make the squid rather special, and funky. And we could all do with more funky squid in our lives.

MEZZE FOR 8

1lb 2oz/500g clean squid
3½ tbsp all-purpose flour
   (or you can use spelt)
1 level tsp salt
½ tsp ground white pepper

generous ¾ cup/200ml orange soda
1 tbsp lemon juice
1 tsp tamarind paste
oil, for frying (soy bean oil is cheap and
   nice with fish)

Cut the tube of the squid into rings and toss it in some flour along with the tentacles.

Sift the rest of the flour and seasoning into a bowl. Mix the soda, lemon juice, and tamarind paste together before beating it slowly into the flour, whisking to achieve a smooth, batter-like paste.

Heat 2in/5cm of oil in a heavy-bottomed pan or, of course, a deep fryer. Once the oil is sizzle-hot, dip the floured squid into the batter, then lower each piece into the oil. Fry for around 3 minutes before removing with a slotted spoon and draining on paper towel. Warning: the batter will be a very dark brown owing to the tamarind—do not panic.

Serve with *Ajvar* (see p.122), or some nice aioli (see bonus recipe on the right—just call me helpful). Cold beer is an optional extra.

SAFFRON AIOLI

Aioli is basically mayonnaise but without the mustard. Another "but" is that it is made with olive oil instead of just vegetable oil. The Spaniards' secret ingredient for a really thick end product is... mashed potato. To make, steep ¼ teaspoon ground saffron in a tiny splash of boiling water. Add the juice of ½ lemon, then either use a whisk or your blender to mix in 1 egg yolk, 4 garlic cloves, and a pinch of black pepper. Slowly add about a scant ½ cup/100ml light extra-virgin olive oil with scant ½ cup/100ml canola or sunflower oil: aiming for a glossy, thick emulsion. Stir in 2 cooked, mashed (cooled) waxy potatoes, beating well, a handful of fresh chopped dill and cilantro, and salt.

NICKY'S SQUID *STIFATHO*:
SQUID COOKED IN INK

Nicky isn't from Snackistan. Actually, she's from Reading in England, but she has an innate feel for food, especially Mediterranean stuff. Which is lucky, since she runs a very busy restaurant kitchen in Walthamstow, northeast London. Walthamstow isn't very near Snackistan either, come to think of it.

Anyway, this recipe evolved during her summers spent working in Greece and many years spent head cheffing in a Cypriot *taverna*. She gets very excited about food, so if you can imagine this recipe recounted with lots of hand gestures and great gusto...

MEZZE FOR 6

a good glug of olive oil

1 bay leaf

about a dozen peppercorns

4 or 5 cloves

1oz/30g cinnamon sticks

2–3 garlic cloves, minced

1lb 2oz/500g squid cleaned, dried and cut up into similar-sized pieces, or if they are babies you can use them whole

scant ¼ cup/50ml red wine

a slosh of red wine vinegar

1 package (around ⅛ oz/4g) squid or cuttlefish ink*

salt

tomato paste, to taste

Tip

I add the salt at the end because sometimes the fish, and the ink, can be quite salty already. The paste helps give a better color (it can sometimes look a bit grey and unappetizing), thickens it slightly, and sweetens it too.

* Squid ink

Oh yes, now about the ink. If you buy fresh whole squid and it's large, you may find ink sacs inside them worth collecting, but the best ink comes from cuttlefish. This can be bought in packets from a fishmonger or you could just make the whole thing with cuttlefish and harvest your own.

Make your saucepan really hot (put it on and leave it while you get your spices and garlic ready) then add the olive oil, quickly followed by the bay leaf, spices, and garlic. Let them fry for a few seconds, being careful because they will pop and spit, then add the squid (which, if you really did heat the pan well, might make quite a frightening noise). Stir briefly, then when all goes quiet, add the red wine, a big splash of vinegar, and the ink. Cover, turn down the heat, and simmer until no longer chewy but still with a bit of bite, anywhere from 20 minutes to 1½ hours depending on the beast in question.

When it's cooked, add salt and a touch of tomato paste to taste and cook for a further 4–5 minutes. Serve with warm bread.

And finally:

Mullah Nasruddin was fishing in a bucket, as one does.
A passer-by stopped out of curiosity and asked the Mullah how many he had caught.
"You are the eleventh," replied Nasruddin, with something akin to a smile playing at his lips.

Meat On Sticks

Mullah Nasruddin bought an okka *(that'll be just over a 2 pounds to you) of juicy meat, on account of having a craving for kebab. He gave it to his wife to cook for dinner later on that day, but while he was out, her girlfriends came over and so she cooked up a kebab feast for them.*

When he got home, he asked the wife if his kebab dinner was ready, only to be told that the cat had gobbled it. Finding it hard to believe that a cat could have eaten so much, he grabbed the animal and put it on the scales. It weighed exactly one okka.

The Mullah scratched his head. "Well this is weird!" he cried. "If this is the same cat that stole my dinner, then where is the meat? And if this is the meat, then where is the cat?"

Kebabs are taken seriously in the Middle East, as the Mullah kindly illustrates in the story above. Iranians are especially fond of them: there's that primeval thing going on with them about cooking meat over fire. During Persian festivities in London, certain of the more spoilsport city councils lock their public parks as they are not amused by the hordes of picnic-barbecuing Iranians who appear. Afghans and Turks too are always barbecuing. I am astonished at the degree of creativity that goes into facilitating the practice: many of my store customers live in high-rise apartments and yet have managed to improvise perfectly ventilated grills on their balconies: I am caught between admiration of their determination and relief that I do not live above them.

And when Snackistanis are out and about, their snack/street food of choice invariably revolves around meat on sticks. Rotating meat on sticks, skewers sizzling over a grill... and kebabs that are fried or baked but are still called kebabs for some reason. The word *kabab* is of Persian origin and originally referred to little bits of fried meat: the word went on a long journey via the steppes thence the courts of Shah Abbas and the Ottomans and thus to nineteenth-century Turkey, where a resourceful guy called Iskender Efendi first devised the vertical grill and came up with the idea of wrapping kebab in bread as handy takeout. A culinary legend was born...

This is not meant to be a streamlined guide to cooking over fire, but a word about skewers is needed. Many of the recipes on the following pages don't need sticks, but if you are skewering food on bamboo sticks, you will need to soak them for around 30 minutes first to stop them flaking. And if you are using metal skewers, don't forget to oil them after use: it prevents rusting and keeps them pristine.

Kebab-e-Koobideh

FEEDS AROUND 6

2 teaspoons (optional:
  see method)

2 medium onions, peeled

2lb 4oz/1kg really good-quality
  ground lamb (shoulder would
  work best: the kebab needs
  some fat in it to make
  it cohere)

2 level tsp salt (Iranians would
  use a lot more)

1 tsp ground black pepper

2/3 tsp baking soda

2 tsp ground cumin (optional)

6 tomatoes, halved

TO SERVE:

6 flatbreads (preferably *lavash*)

ground sumac

This is the most basic-and-yet-popular of the Iranian kebab family. *Koobideh* means ground, and this is indeed a fat skewer of juicy ground lamb. It is perhaps the favorite food of all time among Iranians. Jamshid (husband person) actually dreams about this dish. When he's not dreaming of me, naturally.

The first night I ever spent in my in-laws' home, I was fascinated by the fact that most of their dinner was cooked over a wooden fire in the fireplace, pride of place in the proceedings being given to this *kebab-e-koobideh*. The old fireplace is now covered by a fancy suite, but still when the mood takes them they will invite all the family over, push the furniture back, and host an indoor barbecue.

It is in principle simple, the flavor coming from the correct blend of meat and onion, perfect seasoning, and the fact that it is (ideally) cooked over a real fire. The only complicated part in making it is getting it to stick to the skewers. Iranians love trying to teach the uninitiated how to do it, as it is such a great source of mirth to them. *Koobideh* are traditionally cooked on broad, flat skewers ¾–1¼in/2–3cm in width: if you don't have any flat skewers (most Iranian stores sell them), just use two parallel thin skewers... or you can just do the whole thing without the skewers.

Light the barbecue or preheat the grill or oven to 425°F/220°C. Put the bowl end of 2 teaspoons in your mouth so that they cross over, then grate the onions. This is as close to non-crying as you can hope to get in the weepy world of onions: really, it works.

Mix the onion into the lamb and add the seasoning, baking soda, and cumin, if using. Pound the mixture well with your hands: generally the less you play with food the better, but in this case the mixture benefits from the warmth of your hands, as this causes the fat to soften and the whole thing to come together.

Using wet hands, mold the meat on to your skewers (these kebabs are usually made to around 7in/18cm long), allowing the impression left by your fingers to show—the kebab should still display these wavy crenellations once it's cooked. Throw your skewers on to a hot barbecue, under a hot broiler, or even into the oven on a baking tray. They will need about 5 minutes a side to cook (longer in the oven).

If you don't have any skewers, just form the meat into sausage shapes and use a spatula to lift them onto your grill.

Thread the tomato halves on to (any old) skewers and grill them alongside the meat.

Put a sheet of folded *lavash* (or other bread) on to a plate. As each of the skewers of lamb is cooked, lift the folded over part of the bread over the skewer, pressing it down on top of the kebab. If you exert enough gentle pressure, you should now be able to withdraw the skewer, leaving the kebab nestled in the bread. Add a couple of tomato halves, sprinkle with sumac, then tuck the ends of the bread in to make the kebab more wieldy.

These kebabs are just as often enjoyed with buttered saffron rice, when they become known as *chelow kebab. Noshe jan!* (Which kind of means "enjoy!' and "*bon appétit!*" and "you're welcome!" all in one expression.)

Tip
The secret in eliciting the maximum meaty enjoyment out of this dish is to let the kebab "rest" for around 5–6 minutes after cooking, so that at least some of the juices from the meat soak into the bread. Of course, if you leave it for too long, the thing will become far too soggy.

Jujeh Kebab

SPRING CHICKEN MARINATED WITH LEMON AND SAFFRON

Jujeh kebab is on the menu of every Iranian restaurant and kebab joint across the globe: its flavor is simply stunning and it would be easy to assume there is some trick or secret ingredient involved. There is not. It is truly easy to make, and the learning thereof will greatly enhance your barbecue cred.

This is one's other half's recipe. He is apparently king of the grill. All men believe that they have inherited the barbecue gene: Iranian men reckon they invented it. For this reason, you should never leave them alone with a box of matches: their inner Zoroastrian will come to life. Father-in-law has been found lighting fires (for the most part fairly safely) in the most ill-advised of places. The upside of this national tendency, of course, is that if you are ever shipwrecked with an Iranian male, he will at least be able to light a fire.

SERVES 4

2 poussins (baby chickens), boned, skinned and chopped into 1½in/4cm pieces

2 onions, grated or very finely chopped

½ tsp ground saffron

⅔ bottle Iranian lemon or lime juice (which is somehow extraordinarily strong), or the juice of around 6 fresh lemons or 10 limes

salt and freshly ground black pepper

a dash of olive oil

It's a cinch; all you do is….

Place the chicken in a sealable container and add all the other ingredients. The saffron should be sprinkled onto a saucer of boiling water and allowed to cool before it is mixed in. You only need to add as much lemon juice as it takes to cover the meat, but this probably will be most of the bottle. Mix the ingredients well, cover, and marinate overnight in the fridge.

When you are ready to cook, thread the chicken onto skewers and cook over fire if possible; although you can cook it in the oven (400°F/200°C) on a baking tray for around 20 minutes, or you can broil it for around 15 minutes, turning it from time to time.

Serve wrapped in warm flatbread with a pile of fresh herbs to replicate that downtown Tehran experience. Alternatively, you could always make it dinner food by throwing it on a bed of basmati rice and serving it alongside fresh herbs, pickles, and raw onion.

Kebab-e-Chenjeh
AKA SHISH KEBAB

The story of the origins of *shish kebab* are somewhat apocryphal: the idea of tired and hungry hunters/horsemen roasting chunks of meat on the end of their swords is so logical it must be true, right? *Shish* is actually the Turkish and Armenian word for skewer, although the term *shish kebab* is now widely understood to refer to the dish of cubes of meat (invariably lamb or beef) on a skewer. *Chenjeh* is the Persian term for a kebab of this nature.

You would think that this would be the easiest, shortest recipe in the chapter. Like, put meat on stick and cook it. And it really is that simple... until you start investigating the great salt debate. After a great deal of "serious scientific research" (a euphemism for lots of eating and reading), I have summarized my conclusions about salt and meat below; it should however be remembered that there is no hard and fast rule, as cooking temperatures and cuts of meat vary considerably.

1. Lamb is a fatty meat that benefits from a long and well-seasoned marinating period. A moderate amount of salt added to the mix will aid the breaking down of the fat in the meat and considerably improve the flavor. Seasoning immediately prior to cooking dries and toughens the meat. 2. Beef is less prone to desiccation and can be seasoned in advance or immediately prior to cooking; the latter seems best to enhance the meaty flavor. 3. Salt and souring agents, such as vinegar and lemon juice, do not work well when used together in a marinade, for some very technical reason which failed to impress my tiny brain cell.

So with all of this in mind, and with the utmost of restraint, I offer you my simplest recipe ever.

SERVES 4

1lb 12oz/800g boneless lamb, cubed (loin chops are good—but expensive; leg is standard for kebabs, but our Kashmiri butcher uses shoulder, which, with sufficient marinating, is an excellent and tasty choice)

3 tbsp olive oil

1½ level tsp salt

1 tsp coarsely ground black pepper

TO SERVE:

4 tomatoes

flatbread

lemon wedges

Put the meat into a bowl, add the oil and seasoning, and mix well, before covering the bowl and chilling for 8–24 hours. Remove the meat from the fridge around 20 minutes before you need it: fridge-cold meat often burns on the outside before the inside is cooked.

When you are ready to cook, light the barbecue or preheat your grill or broiler. Thread the cubes on to skewers and cook over hot coals (or under the hot broiler), turning regularly: the meat will need about 6–7 minutes altogether. Halve the tomatoes and thread these on to skewers to cook alongside the lamb.*

Serve the *chenjeh* kebabs with the tomatoes in warm flatbread, accompanied by plenty of lemon wedges and perhaps an herby onion salad.

* Tip on cooking
Everything cooks at different speeds, so tempting though it is to alternate meat and vegetables on one skewer to make it look pretty, it is nearly always best policy to do things the Iranian way and cook the different ingredients separately. The exception is the beef, pepper, and onion combo in the next recipe...

BEEF KABOB, GEORGIAN STYLE

SERVES 4

FOR THE MARINADE:

1lb 12oz/800g sirloin or porter-
   house steak, cut into 1¼
   in/3cm cubes
1 medium onion, grated
4 garlic cloves, minced
1 cup/250ml pomegranate juice
1 tbsp apple cider vinegar
1 tsp cracked black peppercorns
1½ tsp dried thyme
1½ tsp dried oregano
3 bay leaves
2 tbsp olive oil

TO ASSEMBLE:

1 red bell pepper, cut into
   1¼ in/3cm squares
1 yellow bell pepper, cut into
   1¼ in/3cm squares
1 green bell pepper, cut into
   1¼ in/3cm squares
8–12 green chilies (optional)
2 red onions, cut into chunks
pinch of sea salt

If Iran is the Times Square of Snackistan, then Georgia is its Grand Central Station: it is truly at the intersection of the Middle East and Europe. It faces the Black Sea but pokes into Iran and Turkey and extends up into Russia. It is both the snapper-up of unconsidered cultural trifles (courtesy of all the through traffic), and the proud owner of a more or less uncontaminated culinary and linguistic heritage. The nation mostly comprises Orthodox Christians, and was under the Russian thumb for many years, yet the inhabitants (the ones with whom we are acquainted at least) seem more closely allied to Iran than anywhere else.

Fast food seems to be a bit of an anomaly in this nation of feasters: Georgians regard themselves as the inventors of the dinner "toast," and their dinner parties, known as *supra*, are legendary. They comprise what is perhaps the forerunner of the supper club phenomenon: an evening of formal eating and informal drinking, wherein every addition to the repast is heralded by an announcement by the *tamada* or toast master. Beef kabob is perhaps one of their few truly authentic street food recipes.

Cows aren't big in Snackistan. Well, they're probably the same size as cows anywhere else. But they are not the livestock of choice across most of the region.* In Greece, Turkey, Georgia, Armenia, and Kazakhstan, the meat is more popular however, and these kebabs are common street fare.

Put the beef in a bowl, together with all the other marinade ingredients and mix well. Chill for around 6 hours, or overnight.

Remove the meat from the fridge 30 minutes before you want to cook: this allows any marbled fat to warm slightly, which means it will melt readily. Thread the beef cubes on to skewers, alternating with pieces of pepper, chili, and onion (which handily all take the same amount of time to cook). Now is the time to season them with a little sea salt (see note on salt on p.51).

Light the barbecue or preheat the grill or broiler and cook the kebabs, turning them regularly, for around 7–8 minutes, or according to preference.

Serve with flatbreads, lemon, and thick yogurt. These are bad boy kebabs in as much as they smell really appetizing as they cook: be prepared to share with the neighbors...

＊ A note on cows

It is believed that cattle were domesticated as far back as 3,000 BC in Mesopotamia and Egypt, but the animals were used mostly for milk and working in the fields.

AFGHAN *SHAMI KABOB*

A while back, an unusually chubby young Afghan came to do a couple of days' work for us. He rejoiced in the rather splendid forename of Gul-Agha, which means Mr. Flower (this isn't strictly necessary for you to know in order to make kebabs, but it has always made me smile). Anyway, we realized that he wasn't the ideal long-term staff solution that we had been seeking as he looked set to eat his way through all the profits: he never stopped snacking. *Shami kabob* is apparently his favorite fare, and as he remains a good customer, he was happy to elicit and share this recipe from his sister's mother-in-law's neighbor's granny (or some such). There is a shortcut version at the bottom of the recipe.

This isn't really meat-on-sticks, as *shami kabobs* are actually fried. But this very fact makes them easy to make at home. Always make extra as they are perfect to keep in the fridge for grazing teens or abnormally peckish staff.

Put the split peas into a pan with the lamb and onion. Add the potatoes to the pan, together with the cinnamon, cardamom, cloves, ginger, garlic, chili, and just enough water to cover. Bring to a boil, then turn down the heat and simmer for around 1 hour, or until the split peas and the lamb are truly tender.

Drain the mixture, retaining the stock, and fish out the cinnamon sticks. Either mince the meat, vegetables, and remaining spices together, or place it all in the blender along with the egg, cumin, coriander, and salt (if you go for the mincing option, then clearly you should add the egg afterwards). If you are blending the meat, be careful not to over-process it or it will become quite gloopy and unworkable. If the mixture seems too dry, add a little of the reserved stock; if it is too wet, a spoonful of flour usually does the trick.

Chill the "kabob" for 30 minutes–1 hour: this will make it easier to shape. When you are ready to cook, use wet hands to shape the mixture into 3½–4in/9–10cm long sausages (the traditional shape: there is of course nothing stopping you making them any shape or size you like). Heat a little oil in a frying pan and cook the kabobs in batches until they are golden brown, before scooping them out onto paper towel to drain.

Serve wrapped in bread with plenty of fresh herbs, some zinging chutney, raw onion, and lemon wedges.

MAKES ABOUT 12

½ cup/2 ⅓ oz/100g yellow split peas (preferably chana dal)

1lb 2oz/500g lamb (preferably shoulder), boneless and cut into small pieces*

1 onion, quartered

1–2 medium potatoes (around 5½ oz/150g worth), peeled and chopped

2 cinnamon sticks

2–3 cardamom pods, pricked

2–3 cloves

¾ in/2cm piece fresh ginger, peeled and roughly chopped

3–4 garlic cloves, roughly chopped

1 hot green chili, stalk removed

1 egg

1 tsp ground cumin

1 tsp ground coriander

1 tsp salt

* In a hurry?
Just use ground lamb mixed with cooked split peas, boiled mashed potato, grated onion, diced garlic, ginger, and chili. And use pre-ground versions of the spices.

BALUCHI *CHAPLI* KEBABS

FEEDS 4–6 WARRIORS

1 lb 10oz/750g ground lamb
  (traditionally mutton)

3 tbsp roasted chickpea (gram)
  flour

2 tbsp crushed coriander seeds

2 tbsp crushed *anardaneh*
  (or use 1 level tbsp sumac,
  or the grated zest of 2 lemons;
  see note on p.58)

2 tsp ground cumin

3–4 green chilies, chopped
  (or use 1 tsp chili powder)

1 bunch of scallions, very very
  finely chopped

½ bunch of fresh mint, chopped

½ bunch of fresh cilantro,
  chopped

1 egg

3 large tomatoes, cut into
  thick slices

oil, for frying

TO SERVE:

hot flatbreads

raw onion rings

chopped raw chili peppers
  (optional, of course)

lemon wedges

Baluchistan—such a lovely name for a nation. It is a real state (unlike Snackistan, of course, which is an even better name), but so very few people know where or what it is. I only know a bit about it because quite a lot of Baluch seem to live in South London. It is, like Kurdistan, a country without borders, a confederation of Kureishi Arabs (in all likelihood from Syria) and Iranian tribes occupying southeast Iran, southern Afghanistan, and southwestern Pakistan. In Iran and Pakistan there are provinces named accordingly but there is a strong core of Baluch who would like to see their country attain independence.

The Baluch culture is colorful: clothing, music, and literature are full of character. And the cuisine is a delightful mix of the subtlety of Persian and Arabic cuisine with the full-on spices of the lands to the East.

This is one of those lovely recipes that come with a spurious story attached. This then is my re-telling of the great fifteenth-century legend of Sheh Murid and Hani, as recounted by one of my customers...

Yeki boud, yeki na boud *(which is Farsi for "once upon a time"), in the lands bordered to the East by the great, god-like River Indus, and to the South by the sun-dappled Arabian Sea, there lived a young couple. In fact, there lived many young couples, but this is the tale of just one of them. Sheh Murid was a fine and noble lad, famed for his skills with the bow and on horseback. Hani was a young beauty of equally noble lineage, Sheh Murid's childhood playmate, and more recently his betrothed.*

Sheh Murid's closest friend was Mir Chakar, who was also engaged. As good girls who were about to be married could no longer appear before their beloved, for a splendid jape Sheh Murid and Mir Chakar decided to visit each other's fiancées. They were both parched from a long hunting trip: Hani brought Mir Chakar some pure cold water with bits of straw in it, thus forcing him to drink slowly; Sheh Murid, on the other hand, was served a cup of water drawn straight from the well, which he drank quickly and promptly threw up. Mir Chakar realized that Hani was indeed quite a catch.

A week or so later, the young men were at a poetry recital where the epic deeds of Baluch warriors were being fêted. Mir Chakar challenged the assembled great and good to make a promise that very day, which they would then keep for the rest of their lives. Many rash words were spoken that day, which led to one noble being forced to kill his own son, and another to steal his neighbors' camels. Sheh Murid for his part swore that on his wedding day, he would give any guest present anything that they demanded. (Poetry recitals of yore were clearly dangerous affairs.)

The day of Sheh Murid's wedding came around, and, as you have probably guessed, Mir Chakar demanded that Sheh Murid gave him the hand of Hani. Sheh Murid and Hani were both equally devastated by this, but in those days of

extreme chivalry and mad pledges, a man's word was a man's word. Sheh Murid was so distraught that he put aside the trappings of warfare and hunting and eventually took himself off into exile to avoid the torture of seeing his woman at the side of another man.

A long time passed, during which Sheh Murid lived the life of an ascetic, praying and devoting himself to God. One day, many years later, his path took him to the door of Mir Chakar's palace, where he was mistaken for one of the many beggars hanging around the gates waiting for alms. An archery competition was taking place in the town, and the warriors participating couldn't help but notice the grubby tramp who was staring at the contest. Eventually, for a joke, they called him over and offered him a try. So strong was Sheh Murid that he broke the first three bows he handled, and so, intrigued, the nobles summoned forth the great iron bow which had once belonged to "the great Murid Khan," which no one else could even bend. He easily shot three arrows from the weapon, whereupon those assembled realized that Sheh Murid had returned.

It so happened that Mir Chakar had been unable to consummate his marriage to Hani as she remained in love with her childhood sweetheart, and so he gave her leave to reunite with Sheh Murid. Unfortunately, not all fairy tales have happy endings: the latter, touched though he was to see his betrothed one more time, had come to realize that his one true love was God. Legend has it that he subsequently rode off into the sunset on a white camel, as one does, never to be seen again. Sheh Murid is hallowed as a minor saint in Baluchistan.

It is rumored that *chapli kebab* was created in the image of the great hero's shield; others say that it represents the sandals that he used in his wanderings as a holy man (*chapli* means "flat shoe" in Pashto). Whatever the origins of the dish, it remains popular street fare across the region.

Mix all the ingredients (up to and including the egg) for the kebabs together and chill for an hour or so to enable the flavors to mingle.

When you are ready to cook, form the meat into around 12 balls, then flatten and shape them into, well, shield shapes. Press a slice of tomato into the meat one side. Heat some oil in a pan and fry the patties on both sides until golden, taking particular care when cooking them with the tomato side down.

Serve immediately with bread, raw onion, chopped chili, and lemon, and perhaps some yogurt to take care of the heat.

OLIVES WITH WINGS

Versatile though chicken is, it is truly one of my least favorite comestible items. But wings I can always manage. Gotta love chicken wings. It's like the Great Food Designer (assuming one goes with the theory that we are meant to eat meat: but here is not the place to get into that debate) gave us the chicken as meal food, and then added the wings in case we felt like snacking later. They are perfect snack fare—one or two bites and they're gone—and they're so responsive to marination.

I first tried "barbecued" olives in Greece—and was very pleasantly surprised. The charcoal adds a real smokiness to them.

MUNCHIES FOR 4

FOR THE CHICKEN:
8 chicken wings, skin on
1 tbsp Turkish black olive paste (or tapenade)
2–3 garlic cloves, minced
½ tsp ground black pepper
1 level tsp dried rosemary
juice and zest of ½ a lemon

FOR THE OLIVES:
around 24 large green olives, pitted
the other ½ of the lemon (see opposite),
     cut into quarter slices
1 tbsp olive oil
½ tsp dried thyme
2 garlic cloves, minced

Put the chicken in a bowl. Mix all the other ingredients for the chicken together and spoon it over the wings, using your hands to work the marinade into the meat. Cover and set aside for around 30 minutes (out of the fridge will be fine as long as it is only 30 minutes).

Same with the olives: put them in a bowl and add all the other ingredients.

When you are ready to cook, light the barbecue or preheat the grill or broiler. Thread the wings on to skewers and grill for around 3 minutes per side, or until cooked. While they are cooking, wrap the olives (plus marinade) in a foil parcel and put it on the cooler end of the barbecue (or in the oven if you're doing stuff indoors).

Serve hot as a barbecue appetizer or leave in the fridge as a very wholesome anytime snack.

QUAIL ON STICKS

FEEDS 6 AS AN
APPETIZER OR SNACK

1 tsp fennel seeds

2 tsp coriander seeds

1 tsp cumin seeds

3 tsp *anardaneh* (sun-dried
   wild pomegranate seeds,
   optional)*

3 garlic cloves

1 tsp ground ginger

1 tsp ground cinnamon

½ tsp ground chili

3 tsp sea salt

4 tbsp olive oil

6 nice plump fresh quail

Little birds. To the ancients they must have seemed like a limitless source of snack-shaped gifts from Mother Nature. Easy to catch, cook, and eat. Arriving in migratory fashion quite often at precisely the time when other food became scarce. To be fair, they were widely enjoyed in Europe until comparatively recently (remember the four and twenty blackbirds baked in a pie?), and the French were ever partial to brandy-soaked ortolan. But something happened along the historical way, at least in northern Europe: we got conservation-conscious, aware of threatened species, and at the same time the need to catch our own food was removed. Little birds became "cute." Taboo as food. And many of them became protected.

But across the Middle East, no such taboos exist: still to this day songbirds of all shapes and varieties are caught, quite often cruelly, and consumed. The trade in small birds is especially reprehensible in Cyprus, where the dish of *ambelopoulia* is much prized: the birds (mostly blackcaps) are often caught in glue traps. Elsewhere methods are less cruel, but the practice is no less commonplace: in Iran, my in-laws talk of buying bags of (net-caught) assorted little birds from the bazaar to marinate and barbecue—they find my RSPB (Royal Society of Bird Protection) membership and slightly daffy relationship with our local starlings unfathomable.

Anyway, rather than give you a recipe for barbecued bulbul or snack-sized sparrow burgers, here's perhaps a more acceptable one for an easy quail kebab.

Quail somehow have escaped the taboo (sadly this may be because they don't sing and they're not that pretty): they are farmed, readily available in our supermarkets, and "enjoying" renewed popularity on the Western dinner table. They are also hugely popular across Snackistan, from simple supper grills to elaborately stuffed banquet fare. Claudia Roden writes of quail flying south and dropping from exhaustion on beaches in Alexandria, whereupon happy locals would gather them up and gobble them. Recipes for them abound all the way from Morocco to Afghanistan.

*** Anardaneh
(sun-dried wild
pomegranate seeds)**
These seeds add a nice tartness to dishes. They are available in Middle Eastern and Indian stores, but they can be hard to find, so you can leave it out of this recipe or substitute 2 teaspoons ground sumac (which you should then add at the same stage as the chili).

Toast the fennel, coriander, cumin, and *anardaneh*, if using, in a small frying pan until they start hissing at you. Tip them into a mortar and pestle or spice grinder (hey—an old dish towel will do) and pound them. Next add the garlic, ginger, cinnamon, chili, and sea salt and work the ingredients into a paste, slowly trickling in the olive oil.

Now rinse the quail and pat them dry. Butterfly them by cutting along the backbone, opening them out and flattening them with the palm of your hand. Rub the flavored oil all over the birds, cover, and chill for a few hours.

When you are ready to cook, light the barbecue or preheat the grill. Thread each flattened quail on to 2 skewers (threaded about 1½in/4cm apart) and grill them over hot charcoal; 3–4 minutes a side should do the trick. Alternatively, cook them under a hot broiler until done. Serve with flatbread and plenty of lemon wedges; a tomato and onion salad on the side would be nice too.

Gyros
THE PORK AND FRIES GYRO

MAKES ABOUT 10

FOR THE *GYROS*:

2lb 4oz/1kg pork taken from the eye of the shoulder (aka pork neck fillet/ tenderloin, a tender yet flavorsomely fatty cut)

scant ½ cup/100ml red wine vinegar

scant ¼ cup/50ml olive oil

5 garlic cloves, minced

1 tbsp dried oregano

1 tbsp paprika

1 tsp ground cumin

1 tsp cracked coriander seeds

1½ tsp crushed sea salt

1½ tsp crushed black pepper

FOR THE FRIES:

10 potatoes, peeled and cut into thin fries (keep them in water if you are prepping ahead)

olive oil, for frying

TO ASSEMBLE:

1 cup/250ml thick plain yogurt

1½ tbsp English mustard

2 tsp dried dill

salt and freshly ground black pepper

10 slices of pita (try to get the thin round ones if you can)

4–5 firm tomatoes, thinly sliced

1 white onion, thinly sliced

The sandwich that makes the average street-corner *gyro* look like health food. Well maybe that's a slight exaggeration—but this is one chin-dribbling, fatty, cholesterol-laden, glorious snack. The perfect street food munch for when you've had one too many ouzos at the *bouzouki* bar—or when you're having an informal get-together at home. Many of you will have tried *gyros* in Greece: it is *souvlakia*'s fast food cousin. Beguilingly aromatic sizzled pork is crammed into a circular pita pocket with a hefty french fry garnish. *Opa!*

Notwithstanding the fact that few domestic kitchens actually have a vertical grill, it is quite possible to make a pretty decent *gyros* approximation at home. Napkins at the ready?

Using a very sharp knife, cut the pork into thin slices, less than ½in/1cm in thickness, then cut each slice into teensy striplets, around 1½in/4cm in length. Bash the meat with the palm of your hand and set it aside.

Beat all of the other ingredients for the *gyros* together in a bowl before adding the meat and turning it over so that it is thoroughly coated. Tip it into a (hole-free) plastic bag, tie the bag loosely at the top and put it in the fridge. It needs a good 2 hours—overnight would be better still—during which time, turn the meat over in the marinade just by manipulating the bag.

Mix the yogurt, mustard, and dill together with just a dash of seasoning and chill until needed.

When you are ready to cook, preheat the oven to 400°F/200°C. Shallow-fry the potatoes in batches in olive oil and put them in a tray in the bottom of the oven to keep warm. While you are doing this, drain the meat, tip it into a baking tray, and slide it in to cook. It will need only about 15 minutes, so keep an eye on it.

Once the fries are ready and the meat is crispy-cooked, broil or bake the pita bread until it starts to puff up, then make an incision along the side of each piece to form a pocket. Spoon a little of the yogurt sauce into each, along with a few slices of tomato and onion. Use tongs to distribute the meat between the pitas, and dollop a handful of fries artfully into each. Now get your guests to form an orderly line...

Handy knife hint #1: The gentle art of tomato cutting is made considerably easier/ safer if you use a bread/serrated knife. The serrations grip and penetrate the fruit rather than sliding off or squashing it.

Handy knife hint #2: Blunt knives are so much more dangerous than sharp ones: sharp knives will cut with precision; blunt ones are more likely to slide or bounce off the object you are cutting and "collide" with your finger. But you all knew that, right?

THE HOME *SHAWARMA* EXPERIENCE

Shawarma, the ultimate test for a wannabe vegetarian. I don't eat a lot of meat, myself: in fact I could easily give it up tomorrow. Except... except... Oh the greasy-chinned, garlic-sauced, slightly chilied joy of a hot *shawarma kebab* on a cold autumn evening: that is one carnivorous pleasure I could never entirely renounce.

Of all the kebabs in this chapter, this is the one dish that I can't help feeling might be best left as street food, but it is pretty easy to re-create at home. The word *shawarma* is derived from the Turkish verb "to turn," but in truth you don't need an upright spit: this method just needs a griddle or frying pan. And you could always walk up and down in the road outside your house chomping the thing if you really want your *shawarma* experience to feel totally authentic.

Note: this needs 24 hours' marination.

* Mastic

This is funny, chewy, resiny stuff. Gets used in such a worrying range of industries that one is left wondering about its suitability as a foodstuff. It appears mostly in sweet recipes these days, but in Middle Eastern kitchens of yore it was used as an aromatic spice in savory dishes and is mentioned extensively in Al-Baghdadi's thirteenth-century cookbook. It is widely available in Middle Eastern and Greek stores, but you can just leave it out of this recipe: its effect is subtle. To use, take one or two granules and crush them to a powder; you can then use it as you would any other spice.

MAKES AROUND 6,
WITH LEFTOVERS FOR PACKED
LUNCH THE NEXT DAY

FOR THE MARINADE:
2lb 4oz/1kg boneless leg of lamb (or use
    the equivalent weight of boneless
    chicken—roughly 2 birds)
6 garlic cloves, minced
2 tsp ground cinnamon
2 tsp ground allspice
1 tsp ground cardamom
1 tsp ground cumin
½ tsp ground cloves
½ tsp ground nutmeg
1 tsp salt
½ tsp ground mastic (optional)*
generous 1 cup/9oz/250g plain yogurt
    (inauthentic, but for the
    home-experience, yogurt seems
    to bring out a stronger flavor)

3 tbsp apple cider vinegar
2 tbsp olive oil

FOR THE GARLIC SAUCE
(AKA *THOOM*):
1 whole bulb garlic, peeled
big handful of chopped fresh parsley
1 tbsp lemon juice
pinch of salt
¾–1 cup/200–250ml olive oil

TO ASSEMBLE:
3 large *khobez* (Arabic flatbreads,
    like huge pita bread)
Iranian or Arabic pickled cucumbers
    (i.e. spicy ones, not sweet)
Snackistan Patent Kebab Salad
    (see bonus recipe opposite)
hot sauce (optional)

Cut the lamb (or chicken) into narrow striplets, 2½–2¾in/6–7cm in length and just ½–¾in/1–2cm in width. Discard any really tough gristle, but leave all the fat on the meat. Mix the garlic and the spices into the yogurt along with the vinegar and oil; stir well before adding the meat and mixing thoroughly. Cover and chill for 24 hours: you may do the same if you wish.

Next for the *thoom*. This is much easier with a blender. Throw in the peeled garlic, parsley, lemon juice, and salt. Blend well, then very slowly trickle in the olive oil: we are making an emulsion and if you rush it, it will crack/curdle. If you want the sauce thicker, add more olive oil: if it turns out too thick, whisk in some more lemon juice or water. Pour it into a bowl, cover, and chill.

When you are ready to cook, heat your griddle (or barbecue) or frying pan and sizzle the marinated meat in batches: each batch should take just 2–3 minutes, but if you are using chicken, make sure it is cooked through. Put the cooked meat into a warm oven to keep hot until you are ready to wrap and roll.

Warm the *khobez* just a little, then split each piece into 2 discs. Place 1 disc on a board in front of you, then stripe some pickled cuces, and Snackistan kebab salad across its width, just short of the middle, i.e. so that two-thirds of the bread is visible above it and the other third is peeking out on the side nearest your tummy. Spread some of the cooked meat over the wrap, then spoon some of the *thoom* and hot sauce, if using, over it. Now roll the bread up, starting at the shorter end. Once you have rolled as far as the filling, use your little fingers to tuck in the excess bread flaps so that the filling is completely encased in bread. Roll it right up, wrap it in a twist of paper, then repeat with the other discs of bread. Enjoy...

BONUS RECIPE: THE PATENT SNACKISTAN KEBAB SALAD MIX

This is so useful for barbecues: in fact, it will go with just about any hot sandwich, and when I worked at a kebab joint back in the day (yes, I have served my apprenticeship) we got through about 20lbs of this stuff each opening session. Just mix very finely sliced white cabbage with very finely sliced onion. Add some very finely sliced tomato and cucumber halves (i.e. cut into semi-circular slices) and lots of chopped herbs of your choice (mint, parsley, and cilantro are the obvious ones). Add salt and pepper and dress with lemon juice as desired.

BONUS RECIPE: GLUTEN-FREE FLATBREAD

A handy hint for those of you like me whose relationship with wheat has gone sour. You can still enjoy barbecues with flatbread: just make your own. It is very simple: I got this recipe from the lovely Pippa Kendrick in two tweets, thus:

Sally Butcher @PersiainPeckham
@friendlyfood Hiya! You got any good (easy) recipes for gluten-free flatbread?

Pippa Kendrick @friendlyfood
@PersiainPeckham I do! 4oz/110g of flour (or 2oz/55g chickpea/gram flour & 2oz/55g flour), ¼ tsp xanthan gum (essential), salt, 1 tbsp oil, 4–6 tbsp warm water

@PersiainPeckham sift, pour over oil & water and pull together into smooth dough. Griddle them over high heat for 3 mins each side. Makes 2

RABBIT AND FIG KEBABS

SERVES 4

FOR THE RABBIT:

1 nice (albeit headless) rabbit,
    skinned and jointed*

1 tbsp red wine vinegar

2 tbsp date syrup (if you cannot
    find any, use honey instead)

2 tsp harissa paste (p.21)

4 garlic cloves, minced

2 tsp dried thyme

1 heaped tsp ground cumin

1 tsp ground coriander

1 tbsp canola or
    sunflower oil

1 level tsp salt

FOR THE FIGS:

8 small fresh figs (yes, you can
    used canned ones if they
    are out of season)

⅔ cup/5½oz/ 150g *labneh* or
    cream cheese

½ tsp ground cumin

handful of fresh mint, washed
    and shredded

oil

❋ Rabbit

You can use boneless rabbit, but
there is a kind of Neanderthal
appeal in eating any barbecued
meat on the bone.

Rabbit is widely enjoyed around the Mediterranean and across North Africa, but it does not feature so much in the cuisine of Eastern Snackistan. That is not to say that it is not eaten East of Ankara: the rabbit must have seemed like a wild snack back in the day, readily available in the wildest and remotest landscapes, easy to catch, and relatively easy to clean and cook. And it is still consumed across Iran, Iraq, Afghanistan, and all the other -istans. But it is not regarded as a delicacy, and when talking to customers from those parts, they often dismiss it as "peasant fare." Furthermore, some Muslims question whether it is halal or not.

I first enjoyed sizzling, aromatic rabbit kebabs at a midsummer fiesta on a sweltering Manchegan night: I have to confess that this recipe is born of that somewhat seminal experience, but the flavoring owes a bit to Morocco and another bit to Turkey. The dates and figs give this quite a festive feel: perfect fare for a Halloween barbecue perhaps...

First catch your rabbit... or pay a trip to your butcher. Wash the rabbit joints and pat them dry. Mix all the other ingredients together in a bowl, and add the bunny, turning it over so that it is well coated. If you have time, chill for 6 hours, or overnight: if time is limited, score through the flesh on the thicker joints of meat, tip it into a plastic bag with the sauce, and leave it somewhere "ambient" for 30 minutes, or so.

Remove the stalky bit from the figs with a pointy knife, and use a teaspoon to excavate a little of the fig flesh (which you may eat: cook's pickings and all that). Mix the cream cheese with the cumin and the mint, and spoon it into the fig cavities. Next brush the outside of the figs with a little oil, and nestle them into foil, either as a parcel or individually.

When you're ready, light the coals on the barbecue (or preheat your grill or oven—the latter should be set at 375°F/190°C). Rabbit joints take slightly different times to cook, so arrange the coal so that it is hotter at one end. Remove the meat from the marinade (which you should reserve for basting) and shake it to remove any surplus liquid. Skewers aren't essential, although the use thereof does make turning the meat over easier. Generally speaking, the further towards the rear of the rabbit from which a joint comes, the longer it takes to cook: thus you need to put the rear legs kind of over the coals, the saddle (aka middle bit) next to them, and the front legs furthest away from the heat. Thus arranged, the meat should take around 8 minutes per side to cook through: use the reserved marinade to brush on the rabbit if it starts to look dry. If you are cooking in the oven, the rabbit should take about 40 minutes: put the rear legs and saddle in first, and the front legs after 10 minutes.

Throw the figgy foil parcel/s onto the grill and cook for around 6 minutes or until the cheese is piping hot (they will take slightly longer to cook in the oven).

Serve the rabbit and figs with a crisp green salad and some warm flatbread.

EGGPLANT-WRAPPED CHICKEN

MAKES 12

FOR THE MARINADE:

3 plump boneless, skinless
    chicken breasts
3 tbsp plain yogurt
4 garlic cloves, minced
juice and zest of 1 lemon
1–2 tbsp olive oil
1 level tsp ground turmeric
2 tsp Aleppo pepper
    (or substitute 2 tsp paprika
    with a pinch of chili flakes)
½ tsp salt

TO ASSEMBLE:

2 large eggplants
salt
oil
1¼ cups/4½oz/125g grated
    kashkaval cheese (OK—
    Cheddar will do)
handful of fresh mint, shredded
cocktail sticks (or bamboo
    skewers, presoaked
    and halved)
1¾ cups/400ml tomato passata
    (strained tomatoes)
    or juice

This is a quintessentially Turkish dish, as it comprises the two ingredients without which no Turkish chef can cook: yogurt and eggplant.

I saw something like this on sale in a bustling takeout place in the touristy part of Turkey, but as we had two petulant teens in tow I was not allowed to stop and indulge. This is my effort to recreate the dish back home, although I will now of course just have to imagine the softly lapping Mediterranean, the moon rising across the bay, the smell of herbs and kebabs hovering over the port, and the gentle sound of bickering stepchildren.

Lay each chicken breast flat, then slice through them horizontally so that you end up with 4 very thin slices from each one (a nice butcher might do this for you). Beat the yogurt with all the other marinade ingredients, then immerse the chicken in the mixture. Chill for at least 2 hours; 6–8 would be better.

When you are ready-ish to cook, slice the eggplants thinly lengthways: again you need 12 slices. Rub each slice with salt and leave pressed between some sheets of paper towel for around 20 minutes. At the end of this time, wipe the eggplants dry, then fry them in hot oil just until they are soft and floppy. Drain them on more paper towel and allow them to cool just a little.

Preheat the oven to 400°F/200°C.

Place a slice of eggplant in front of you and sprinkle it with grated cheese and a sprinkle of mint. Remove a chicken slice gently from the marinade and layer it on top of the eggplant, then roll the whole thing up into a sausage. Secure the bundle with a cocktail stick and repeat with the rest of the slices. Place the eggplant rolls in an ovensafe dish, and pour the passata around them. Bake uncovered for 15 minutes; then cover with foil and cook for a further 15 minutes.

Serve the parcels with a diced tomato, onion, and cucumber salad (or the Salata Duco, see p.135), some yogurt, and hot pita bread. And don't forget to remove the cocktail sticks before digging in.

Meat Not On Sticks

The fox prostrated himself during namaz *(prayers),*
then he said, "This fat cow, oh Elect Sultan, is your
mid-morning snack. And a stew can be made for
the goat for the blessed Sultan to eat at midday.
As for the rabbit, it will make a fine titbit for
his kindness and beneficence the Sultan in the
evening... " (Rumi)

The kitchens of Snackistan offer some of the most
creative uses of meat in the world. (Conversely of
course, Middle Easterners are gifted at making
meals out of just a few bones or vegetables in times
of hardship.) No part of an animal is allowed to go
to waste, a culinary ethos that puts our consumer
and convenience-led shopping society to shame,
but I won't dwell on that.

It is of course true that since the rise of Islam
and the conversion of most inhabitants of the
region, the range of meat consumed has shrunk.
Pork is obviously *haram* (taboo), and there is
confusion over the status of many other animals.
So basically we're talking lamb and chicken,
with beef coming a close third, and wildfowl,
waterfowl, and game rare additions to the diet.
To my mind, that makes them chicken and lamb
specialists (and explains the heavy bias of the
recipes in this chapter).

MOTHER-IN-LAW'S *TAS KEBAB*

COMFORT FOOD
FOR 4–6

2 onions, sliced

1 leek, roughly chopped

3 sticks of celery, cut into
  fat chunks

1 chicken, skinned and cut into
  8 pieces

1 tsp ground turmeric

1 tsp lime powder

salt and freshly ground
  black pepper

2 carrots, cut into fat sticks

1 green bell pepper, cut
  into chunks

6–8 mushrooms, wiped

½ small butternut squash, peeled
  and cut into chunks

3 medium waxy potatoes, peeled
  and cut into slabs

1 large eggplant, cut into
  ¾ in/ 2cm cubes

1 cup/7oz/200g prunes (soaked
  if necessary)

2 tbsp good tomato paste

1 can (14oz/400g) chopped
  tomatoes

1 tbsp olive oil

around 1 glass water

Tas kebab is one of those funny recipes that rumbles around the kitchens of the Middle East with no one quite knowing from whence it came. It is a popular and homey dish in countries from Bulgaria all the way around to the Levant, with a small detour to Iran. Even the name is a puzzle: as we noted at the beginning of the previous chapter, originally *kabab* denoted fried chunks of meat with a sauce, which was kind of casserole-ish. *Tas kebab* is just that: a juicy baked meat dish bearing little resemblance to the doner kebabs we know and love/despise.

Every country/province/village/household makes it differently, but the principles are the same: meat or chicken is layered with vegetables and fruit and baked in a fragrant tomato sauce. In Turkey, *tas* means bowl, and *tas kebab* is usually prepared contained within an inverted bowl in the oven: the Persian version we offer here is much simpler. Unlike most of the *khoreshts* (stews) of Iran, *tas kebab* is usually eaten with bread as a comforting supper: the leftovers make for great anytime snack food. It is hearty fare, but economical, as the ingredients are varied according to season and market price. I usually make it with the leftover pieces of vegetables in the bottom of the fridge. It is lovely with cooking apples or quince, when they are available. My mother-in-law normally uses chicken (as here), but occasionally she will prepare it with baby lamb *kufteh*.

My, this is easy. But I might have mentioned that already. Preheat the oven to 375°F/190°C.

Layer the onions, leek, and celery into the bottom of a fairly deep baking tray. Arrange the chicken on top and sprinkle it with the spices and seasoning. Dot the rest of the vegetables and the prunes evenly around and on top of the chicken.

Mix the tomato paste, tomatoes, and olive oil together, and add the cold water. Pour the liquid over the chicken and vegetables, cover the tray properly with foil, and bake for around 1 hour 10 minutes, or until the chicken is cooked through and the vegetables are tender. Serve with warm bread.

Dizzee

MASHED LAMB WITH STOCK

This isn't quite street food, but it is served at truck stops up and down Iran: it is the favorite fare of Persian truck drivers. It is also probably Iran's favorite comfort food. I once tried to serve this to guests and my mother-in-law looked at me with as much horror as if I had been dishing up dinner in my PJs: this is schlepping around the house food, not fancy food.

Dizzee was historically (and may still be) a way of stretching a few meager bones into a nourishing meal. The idea is that lamb is bubbled away with potatoes and beans and (usually) dried limes until it literally falls off the bone. The meat is stripped from the bone and mashed up with the taters/beans (using a special meat tenderizer known as a *gusht coup*), while the stock (and the bones: the lamb marrow is one of the best parts, and if you don't want it, save it for me) is served alongside in a mini tureen called a *dizzee* (whence the dish gets its name).

The stock, which is known as *ab gusht* ("meat-water"), can be eaten as a soup; it should also be mentioned that the meat is sometimes left in the stock and relished as an accompaniment to rice.

Place the lamb in a pan with the chopped onions and dried limes. If you are using dried beans, rinse and add them now. Cover with water so that the surface of the liquid is about 2in/5cm above the meat (only ¾in/2cm if you are using canned beans), sprinkle in the turmeric, and bring to a boil. At this stage, you may want to skim the surface of the water: both the beans and the lamb are prone to producing scum/foam. Turn down the heat and simmer the *ab gusht* for around 1½ hours.

After this time, lower the potatoes in; if you are using canned beans, add these now together with the tomato paste. Check that the meat is still covered by the stock (add a little boiling water to top it up, if necessary), and only now should you add some seasoning to taste. Cook for another 30 minutes, or until the potatoes are just starting to disintegrate.

Drain the *ab gusht* through a sieve, retaining every last drop of that lovely stock. Using a fork, pull the meat away from the bones and return any of the bones that are likely to contain marrow to the stock. The dried limes can be discarded at this stage, although hardcore Iranians would probably eat them.

Ideally you should give each person a little bowl of stock, a pile of the cooked lamb/beans/potatoes, and a *gusht coup* so they can mash it themselves. In practice you may want to pound the lamb yourself (so that it is mashed, not puréed), and dish it up family style, with the stock in a separate bowl. *Dizzee* needs lots of warm bread to accompany it: I also rather like frying off some cubed stale bread and floating it into the *ab gusht*. Serve with pickles, yogurt, and raw onion wedges.

SERVES 8

1 shoulder of lamb, trimmed and chopped on the bone into 1½ in/4cm cubes

2 medium onions, chopped

8–10 dried limes, pricked

½ cup/3½ oz/100g chickpeas, soaked overnight (or use 1 can/14oz/400g)

½ cup/3½ oz/100g dried lima beans (or cannellini), soaked overnight (or use 1 can/ 14oz/400g)

2 tsp ground turmeric

4 medium potatoes, peeled and cut in half

1 heaped tbsp tomato paste

salt and freshly ground black pepper

Halim

A RAMADAN/STREET BREAKFAST

TO FEED HALF THE
STREET. WELL, 6–8
PEOPLE AT LEAST

scant 2⅓ cups/1lb 2oz/500g
    pot barley

1 medium skinless chicken

1 tsp ground turmeric

½ tsp (or so) salt

butter

ground cinnamon

sugar

Meat porridge. Hmm. This at first seems to be the weirdest dish; in fact, it remains so at second and third… that is, if you have been raised on Quaker Instant (it goes without saying that if you have been raised on chicken porridge, it tastes quite normal). But it is utterly delicious, and combines a double whammy of comforting carbohydrate with the culinary hug that chicken soup gives you.

Halim is in fact made across most of Snackistan: in Pakistan, it is a spicy dish made with puréed beef, while in Armenia it is a paste that is eaten with bread. In Arabic countries, it is more often known as *harisseh* (which just means "well-cooked"). I offer you the Persian version as it is the simplest.

In Iran, it is eaten as a hearty breakfast (it is in fact so satisfying that it is also great for lunch or dinner), especially in the bazaars of the land, and is most popular during Ramadan. While it is made at home, it is first and foremost street food: children are often sent out to *halim* vendors with empty bowls at the crack of dawn to fetch enough to feed the family. Three points to note: firstly, most Iranians make this dish with wheat instead of barley, but in truth they are largely interchangeable; secondly, they would always use a processed grain, but as most of the goodness is in the husk, we prefer to leave it on; thirdly, the dish is also nice (and more traditional) with lamb or turkey.

Soak the barley for 3–4 hours.

Place the chicken in a large pan, cover with plenty of water, add the turmeric and salt and boil for around 1 hour. Strain off the stock and trim all the flesh from the chicken, giving just a little bit to the cat so that he leaves you alone for 5 minutes.

Put the barley in the pan together with the water in which it has been soaking; add the strained chicken stock and the flaked chicken. Bring to a boil, then turn down the heat and simmer for at least 2 hours (in Iran, they would get up before dawn to get this dish underway, but if you are having it as breakfast we recommend making it the day before). Check it at regular intervals—you may need to add a drop of boiling water if the liquid content is insufficient. The barley is cooked when it is soft and gloopy. When you are happy that this is the case, take off the heat and add more salt to taste. Now comes the fun part—traditionally you would pound this with a mortar and pestle, but to be perfectly honest we just throw it all in the blender. Return the gloop to the pan (it should have a slightly reluctant pouring consistency) and warm through.

To serve, melt some butter (around 3 tablespoons/1½oz/40g per bowlful) in a saucepan and let it simmer until it starts to darken and hiss. Ladle the *halim* into bowls and drizzle a little butter on top of each; sprinkle each with cinnamon and 2 teaspoons sugar. If you are not eating it all at one sitting, it will keep in the fridge for around four days; just make sure that you sizzle your butter freshly every time.

CHICKEN LIVER WITH POMEGRANATE SAUCE

OK, so I thought my husband had flipped when he came up with this little "snackeroony" one evening. Turns out that it's the specialty of one of the (Syrian) restaurants that we supply, and the chef had made a bit extra for him one evening. Jamshid liked it so much he rushed home and made it for me.

It is the perfect fare for those not too fond of the peculiarly earthy flavor of liver: used in moderation, pomegranate paste works as an agent to mask strong odors and tastes in food. Of course, if you use too much you can kill a dish at 20 paces.

SERVES 4 AS A *MEZZE* DISH
OR 1 HUNGRY HUSBAND
olive oil, for cooking
2 garlic cloves, minced
9oz/250g fresh chicken livers (preferably
    organic or those sourced from
    free-range birds)

1 hot green chili, or to taste
2–3 tbsp pomegranate molasses
pinch of sea salt
generous handful of fresh parsley,
    chopped
khobez (Arabic flatbread), to serve
squeeze of lemon, to serve

Heat the oil in a pan, toss in the garlic, and after a few seconds add the chicken livers and chili. Stir constantly for a few moments more before stirring in the pomegranate molasses and adding a little salt to taste. The chicken livers should be just cooked/slightly pink in the middle: overcook them and they will taste like a grubby eraser. Take off the heat and cover with the chopped parsley.

To serve, heat the *khobez* through, slide it onto a plate, and pile the liver on top. Add a squeeze of lemon and the dish ends up with a perfect balance of sweet and sour and umami and salt and bitter (really—it has everything).

FRIED BRAINS IN A SAFFRON SAUCE

They do like a them some brain in Snackistan (notwithstanding the small percentage of citizens therein who believe that eating animal brains destroys the human brain). And brain does make a delicious snack. Wussy Westerners may recoil in horror, but until the last century (when most of us became terribly spoiled) they were widely enjoyed across the West, and in parts of the US, fried brain sandwiches are still a popular fast food option.

Egyptian and Lebanese chefs prepare the dish by frying it in breadcrumbs, but I quite like the simplicity (and butteriness) of this (mostly Persian) offering.

MEZZE FOR 4
2 lambs' brains or 1 calf's brain
1 tbsp lemon juice
1 tbsp flour
salt and freshly ground black pepper
11 tbsp/5½ oz/150g butter

juice and grated zest of 1 lemon
¼ tsp ground saffron steeped in boiling water
1 large sprig of fresh tarragon
   (or 1 level tbsp dried)
big handful of fresh parsley, chopped

Soak the brains in cold water for around 1 hour, then remove any "nasty parts" together with the outer membrane. Next blanch them in boiling water with the 1 tablespoon lemon juice for about 15 minutes before draining and leaving them until cool enough to handle.

Spread a tablespoon or so of flour out on a plate and season it with salt and pepper. Slice the slightly cooled brains into 8 strips and roll them in the flour. Melt the butter in a frying pan and fry the brain slices, turning regularly, for a few minutes. Add the lemon juice and zest, saffron, and herbs, then sizzle for 30 seconds more and take off the heat.

Serve on top of toasted pita or *khobez* (Arabic flatbread) with extra lemon wedges and a little bowl of sea salt. You know what? This stuff tastes a lot better than it looks.

SAUSAGE *BÖREK*
(TURKISH-STYLE SAUSAGE ROLLS)

Sausage rolls. I can't be doing a book about snacks without featuring this most user-friendly form of street fare, except... they're very British, no? A staple of main-street bakers and dire buffet parties the length and breadth of Englistan. Well, no, not really. Pie of sorts was around in ancient Sumer and Egypt, although the Ottomans were probably the first to start wrapping sausage-shaped meat in pastry. And these *böregi* bear very little resemblance to our greasy-but-wholesome pork offerings. And at this stage, I have to confess that it is quite hard to write about sausage rolls without inadvertently creating a childish-giggle moment, but I will aim for restraint.

Börek, burek, böregi, brik: yup, they're basically all the same idea— Snackistani pies, enjoyed all the way from Tunis to Turkistan, made using *yufka* or filo pastry. They come in a wide range of shapes and flavors, and can be baked, fried, or even boiled. Ours are to be baked because the sausage filling is already naughty enough without frying them in more fat.

Preheat the oven to 350°F/180°C.

It is easiest to make the "sausage meat" in a blender. Just throw the garlic, onion, salt, *salçasi*, spices, and parsley into the blender and whizz until the vegetables are finely minced. Add the ground lamb and pulse it again so that everything becomes quite homogenized. If you don't have a blender, just chop it manually, then mix it by hand: the more you pound the meat with your hands, the more the warmth therein will help the mixture adhere.

Work with one sheet of filo at a time, keeping the rest covered with a damp dish towel—the stuff dries out fiendishly fast, and this renders it unusable. Place the pastry on a clean work surface (shorter side towards your tummy) and brush it with the melted butter/oil. Turn it over, then cut it into 4 oblongs. Roll a little sausage mix into a sausage shape (around 2¾–3¼in/7–8 cm long), then place it near to but running parallel with the shorter side (nearest to you) of one of the rectangles. Roll the pastry over the meat (i.e. away from yourself) ¾in/2cm, then tuck in the overhanging pastry flaps on each side. Roll it away from you so that the lamb is completely encased by pastry. Repeat with the other 3 rectangles, then with the other 4 sheets of pastry.

Whisk the eggs, yogurt, and milk together and brush each of the *böregi* with the resulting "glaze" before arranging them on a lightly oiled baking tray. Bake your "sausage rolls" for around 30 minutes, or until golden brown.

Enjoy hot or cold. They are particularly snackable with a bowl of *Ajvar* (see p.122) on the side, and perhaps a very cold bottle of beer to wash it all down.

MAKES 20

3 garlic cloves, peeled

1 small onion, cut into chunks

1 generous tsp salt

1½ tsp hot *biber salçasi* (Turkish hot pepper paste: use the much-easier-to-find harissa in its place if you like)

1 heaped tsp dried marjoram (or oregano)

1 tsp ground cinnamon

1 tsp ground cumin

small bunch of fresh parsley, roughly chopped

1lb/450g fatty ground lamb (if you have a nice butcher get him to grind some lamb shoulder for you without removing too much fat)*

10 sheets of *yufka* or filo (phyllo) pastry

1½ tbsp/¾ oz/20g melted butter mixed with a dash of oil

2 eggs

1 tbsp plain yogurt

splash of milk

✴ Handy hint

If you are in a hurry, skip making your own filling and use the same weight of good-quality pre-made sausages: just snip off the end of the sausage casings and squeeze the sausage meat out. You can then mix it with the spices/herbs/garlic... or not, depending on how much of a rush you're in.

Andreas' Sheftalia
CAUL-WRAPPED MEATBALLS

I've been making these moist and wholesome meatballs for years, but to get the perfect, authentic lowdown I sent my brave, self-sacrificing husband out to play *takhte-nar/tavoli/*backgammon and drink coffee with our Cypriot Ealing crowd connections. Quite a few hours later, he came back with sheets of scribbled notes and a furrowed brow: the Cypriots do like a good debate, especially when food is involved. Sisters and mothers had been consulted, and there had been a lot of hand-waving.

The recipe is a hybrid via Alkis and Andreas. Andreas has been in catering all his life and knows pretty much everything there is to know about snacking, especially meat snacking. He is the only man I know who can turn a plate of discarded cooked chicken bones and a scrap of bread into a feast fit for Olympus.

The traditional way to make *sheftalia* would involve 7oz/200g each ground pork and lamb, plus 3½oz/100g chopped pork fat, but most homecooks these days just use fatty ground pork.

TO FEED 4

1lb 2oz/500g coarsely ground pork
   (neck end is best: it needs to be fatty)
1 large onion, finely chopped
1 bunch fresh parsley (including stalks),
   chopped
⅓ tsp each salt and freshly ground
   black pepper
1 tsp ground cinnamon
3½oz/100g *banna* or pork caul fat
   (fancy name = *omentum*)

Light the barbecue or preheat the grill.

Mix all the ingredients except the caul fat together, pounding well with your hands so that the fat starts to soften.

Stretch the caul fat out, marveling at its weird texture, then cut it into 16 x 2–2½in/ 5–6cm squares. Take a small lump of the meat mixture, roll it into a small fat sausage shape, and place it in the middle of one of the caul squares. Pull the caul fat up around the meat— the stuff is conveniently self-sealing—and repeat with the rest of the mixture.

Sheftalia only really works on charcoal, as the caul fat comes into its own when exposed to direct heat, basting and sealing in the flavor as it melts: cook for 20 minutes, turning them often. You can cook them indoors if it really isn't barbecue weather: poach them in boiling water for around 10 minutes, then put them in a really hot oven preheated to 425°F/220°C (or under a really hot broiler) for another 10 minutes.

Serve with bread and lots and lots of lemon wedges.

Bekri Meze

DRUNKEN *MEZZE*

Now I always thought this recipe was named after the often-inebriated chef who first showed me how to make it. Turns out it's a well-known *mezze* standby, which derives its name simply from the amount of booze that gets added to it. It takes a good 1½ hours to cook, but it is the ultimate "throw it all in the pan and forget about it" dish.

SUPPER FOR 4 OR *MEZZE* FOR 8

2lb 4oz/1kg boneless shoulder of pork, cut
    into ¾–1¼in/2–3cm cubes

flour

1 large onion, chopped

2 bell peppers (why not choose the color
    to match your table linen?), chopped

1 tbsp butter and a dash of oil

3–4 garlic cloves

1 level tsp allspice

1½ tsp dried oregano

1 tbsp tomato paste

about a ⅓ of a bottle of red wine (a good
    chance to use up non-vintage cheap wine;
    dry-ish is better)

6–7 fresh tomatoes, peeled (or 1 can/
    14oz/400g thereof)

2 bay leaves

big handful of fresh parsley, chopped

salt and freshly ground black pepper

Roll the cubes of pork in some flour. Next, fry the onion and peppers in the butter/oil mixture. Once they have softened, add the garlic followed by the meat, stirring constantly, then follow this 10 minutes later with the allspice and oregano. After a minute or so more, mix in the tomato paste, wine, and tomatoes. Bring to a boil, add the bay leaves and parsley, turn down the heat, and simmer, stirring from time to time.

After 45 minutes, season to taste, adding a little cold water if the sauce is too thick or looks dry. Cook for another 30 minutes until the pork is at the point of falling apart (i.e. utterly "drunk"), then serve with bread and perhaps a glass of wine on the side...

Chorba Frik
ALGERIAN STREET SOUP

This is a bit like the Moroccan *harira*, but with meat. Simple-but-filling, spicy soups like this are especially popular during Ramadan and are common street fare during that month. The word *chorba* just means soup, and is used in differently spelled incarnations all the way from Kyrgyzstan to the Maghreb.

Freekeh is green smoked wheat: it is available in good Middle Eastern stores (I can recommend one if you're willing to travel!*), but you can easily substitute barley, which takes about the same time to cook.

SERVES 6

½ cup/3½ oz/100g dried chickpeas
    (or use 1 can/14oz/400g)
1 large onion, diced
splash of oil, for frying
12oz/350g finely diced lean lamb
2 sticks of celery, finely chopped
1 carrot, grated
2–3 garlic cloves (although this is often
    avoided during Ramadan itself as it
    a) makes you thirsty, and b) is deemed
    disrespectful to smell of food during
    the month of fasting)

1 tsp ground cinnamon
½ tsp ground black pepper
½ tsp ground turmeric
6½ cups/1.5 liters water
1 tbsp tomato paste
4½ oz/125g *freekeh*
6 tomatoes, skinned and chopped
    (or use 1 can/14oz/400g)
1 small bunch of fresh cilantro, chopped
salt

Soak the chickpeas overnight (or at least for 6 hours), then drain.

Fry the onion in some oil, then add the lamb and celery, stirring well. When the lamb is sealed all over and the celery has begun to soften, add the carrot, garlic, and spices together with the drained chickpeas (if using dried); after a few minutes more, pour in the cold water, bring to a boil, then turn down the heat and simmer for about 1¼ hours, or until the meat and chickpeas are just cooked.

Next, add the tomato paste, *freekeh*, and chopped tomatoes (together with the chickpeas if using canned) and return to a gentle boil, adding a little more water if the *chorba* looks too thick. Cook for another 30 minutes, or until the wheat is tender. Stir in the cilantro, add salt to taste, and serve immediately.

* Tip
Nepotism aside, do see our list of suppliers on the Snackistan website.

AFI'S LAMB ROULADE

**INFORMAL SUPPER
FOR 4–6**

FOR THE SHELL:

2lb 4oz/1kg ground lamb

1 large onion, grated

½ tsp ground cumin

1 tsp ground cinnamon

1 tsp ground turmeric

1 egg

2 tbsp breadcrumbs

salt and freshly ground
    black pepper

FOR THE FILLINGS:

8 baby carrots, scrubbed,
    topped, and tailed

4 eggs

1 bunch of fresh cilantro,
    chopped

AND

1 big bunch of spinach

1 cup/3½ oz/100g walnut
    halves, crumbled

4oz/125g pitted dried sour
    cherries or prunes

FOR COOKING:

flour (Afi uses chickpea/gram
    flour, but all-purpose flour
    will do)

splash of oil

2 tbsp tomato paste

1 tbsp lemon juice

1¾ cups /14fl oz/400ml
    chicken stock or water

Afi is my mother-in-law. She's over 70 now, but looks a good 20 years younger, and rules her little Peckham/Persian roost with tenacity, generosity, humor, and a rod of iron. We get on famously, and in this I am very lucky, because Iranian mothers-in-law are notoriously pernickety, worthy of every mother-in-law joke in the book and worse.

Afi has been cooking this dish for many years and has made it quite her own, but I think it was originally based on a recipe by Rosa Montazami and the name indicates French origins (Iran has a history of trading with the French dating back to the sixteenth-century Safavid empire). It is one of the few dishes that my father-in-law will agree to eat without a mountain of rice on the side: it's usually enjoyed with bread, yogurt, and fresh herbs.

Preheat the oven to 400°F/200°C.

Firstly, mix the lamb and all the other shell ingredients together, working the meat to blend all the flavors.

For the first filling, boil the carrots whole so that they are a bit more than *al dente*. Hard-boil the eggs (10 minutes with a splash of vinegar works for me) and peel them. Take half the meat mixture and form it into 2 fat sausages. Split them lengthways and arrange the whole carrots, whole eggs, and chopped herbs in the cavity thus created so that every bite and slice will look pretty. Mold the meat back to cover the hidden filling.

For the second filling, steam or stir-fry the spinach for just a few seconds. Take the rest of the ground mixture and, again, make it into 2 fat sausages, this time filling it with spinach, walnuts, and fruit.

Roll each of the meat sausages gently in flour, then fry them in a little oil just to seal them. Next place the lightly browned roulades in a baking pan. Blend the tomato paste with the lemon juice and stock and pour it over the roulades: they should be half covered with sauce.

Cover the dish with foil and bake for 45–50 minutes. Slice thickly and serve. And there you go: Persian meatloaf—a perfect midweek supper.

Dolmeh-ye-Aloo Siah
LAMB-STUFFED PRUNES

Prunes are so often used in stuffing for meat and vegetables that it is rather nice to see them get their own back by being the main feature in this dish.

Stuffing is a big thing in the Middle East, with anything and everything from vine leaves to carp being filled with an astonishing and creative selection of pastes and pilafs. Sometimes one vegetable is filled with different stuffings, sometimes a range of vegetables are all filled with the same stuffing. Sweet, sour, rice-based, wheat-based, crunchy, soft—it's a whole sub-genre of cooking.

If you want to play, you could make a bit more of the stuffing recipe below and bake a range of fruit *dolmeh*: dates, peaches, nectarines, apples, plums, and persimmons would all respond well. Just a thought: I'm not actually trying to create more work for you or anything.

MEZZE FOR 4–5
OR CANAPÉS FOR 20

FOR THE STUFFING:
1 tbsp raisins
1 small onion, finely chopped
splash of oil
½ in/1cm piece fresh ginger, peeled
   and chopped
7oz/200g ground lamb
½ tsp ground turmeric
1 level tsp ground cinnamon

1 tsp dried mint
salt and freshly ground black pepper
1 can (14oz/400g) chopped tomatoes
1 tbsp pine nuts (or use slivered almonds
   or chopped pistachios)
big handful fresh parsley, chopped

TO ASSEMBLE:
20 fat, juicy, pitted prunes
1 tbsp honey
1 tbsp vinegar
big handful fresh mint, shredded

Preheat the oven to 350°F/180°C.

Soak the raisins in a little cold water. Next, fry the onion in a splash of oil. When it softens, add the ginger and the lamb, mixing well. Once the lamb has started to color, add the spices, mint, and some seasoning along with quarter of the can of tomatoes. Simmer for a few minutes, stirring constantly, then add the pine nuts, drained raisins, and parsley and take off the heat.

Spread the prunes out in a small baking tray, and use a teaspoon to insert a spoonful of the meat mixture into each one. Whisk the rest of the canned tomatoes together with the honey and vinegar, and pour this "sauce" into the base of the baking tray. Cover the dish with foil and bake for 30 minutes. Remove from the oven and sprinkle with the shredded mint. These *dolmeh* are best enjoyed hot or at room temperature, and will keep for 2–3 days in the fridge.

JELLIED CHICKEN SALAD

Aspic Schmaspic. And I don't do gelatine either (it just won't dissolve for me, and clumps petulantly at the bottom of whatever I cook). But this easy, economical little recipe is a summer snacker's delight, and makes for an intriguing yet elegant *mezze* dish.

I have a theory that many people don't buy chicken with much forethought. Obviously free-range birds are better all around, but I am talking basic home economics here. Regardless of the cut that you need for a particular dish, it is always more cost-efficient to buy a whole chicken (even if you don't have a stock-pot constantly bubbling on your woodstove), and good butchers will cut it/bone it for you as required. The point being that this recipe is a good way to use any leftover parts of the bird in question.

It is based on something my wonderfully eccentric grandmother used to make. She had an abnormal fascination with "things in jello": of course, as a child I really didn't want to know what lay beneath, but as an adult I have come to realize that she was an extraordinarily good cook. There is an added pinch of Claudia Roden for good measure.

A FUNKY LITTLE *MEZZE* FOR 4–6

1 small chicken (or leftover joints), skin-on
1 small onion, chopped
1 stick of celery, chopped
1 level tsp ground turmeric
salt and freshly ground black pepper
4 dried limes (or 1 small lemon, quartered)
1 tbsp dried dill
⅓ tsp ground saffron dissolved in a splash of boiling water
big handful of fresh parsley, finely chopped

Put the chicken in a pan with the onion, celery, turmeric, salt, and pepper, adding enough water to three-quarters-cover the bird. Bring to a boil, then prick the dried limes (or lemon) and drop them into the pan along with the dill. Turn down the heat and simmer for about 1½ hours, keeping an eye on the liquid levels (which should be allowed to reduce by about half) and turning the chicken over from time to time. When the chicken is visibly falling off the bone, check the seasoning of the stock and take the pan off the heat.

Strain the stock into a bowl and whisk in the saffron and chopped parsley. When the meat is cool enough to handle, strip the skin off the chicken and discard. Pull the meat from the bones and arrange it in a serving dish; then pour the cooling stock over the chicken and cover. Chill overnight, during which time it will set to become a wibbly-wobbly chicken salad. If you don't like the look of the fatty bits on the surface, they can be dabbed off with a piece of paper towel.

Serve with pickles and a robust brown bread.

Zalatina

AKA BRAWN

This is another of Granny Jojo's secret recipes, but with added Cypriot touches. *Zalatina* is widely enjoyed as a snack/*mezze* in Cyprus, and it is a great little number to have in the fridge for summer picnicking. Jojo used to make loads and then distribute it all around the family/bridge club: obviously if you have a squeamish family or don't play bridge, just cut down the quantities accordingly.

In Cyprus, the dish was originally made by country folk as a waste-not-want-not way of using up all parts of a slaughtered pig. You can in theory use all manner of pig parts, but I have suggested ingredients that will be more readily available.

MAKES ABOUT 2LB 4OZ/1KG

1 pig head, or 4 trotters/pig's feet
   (or a combination of both)
1lb 2oz/500g neck end of pork, cut into cubes
2 leeks, chopped
2 sticks of celery, chopped (optional)
3–4 cinnamon sticks
2 bay leaves
6–7 black peppercorns
2–3 tsp salt

1 cup/250ml white wine vinegar
1 cup/250ml lemon juice

TO GARNISH (OPTIONAL):

sliced olives
gherkins, sliced
radishes, thinly sliced
fresh parsley sprigs

Alrighty, the pig's head. Get your butcher to remove the ears and shave as much of the hair from the head as possible. When you get home, wash the head thoroughly: pay special attention to sluicing out the nostrils. If you are using trotters, get the butcher to remove any hair (or do it yourself: burning it off with a match or lighter is the easiest option).

Place the head/trotters in a large pan and cover with water. Bring to a boil, turn down the heat, and simmer for 10 minutes, then drain, before placing the meat back in the pan. Cover with fresh water, adding the neck end of pork, leeks, celery, spices, herbs, peppercorns, and salt. Return to a boil, turn down the heat, and simmer for about 3 hours.

At the end of this time, strain the cooking stock into a fresh pan. Add the vinegar and lemon juice and bubble so that the amount of liquid reduces by half. Set the stock aside to cool: meanwhile, pick all the meat off the bones and cut into roughly equal-sized pieces.

You will need 2 regular-sized (1lb 2oz/500g) meatloaf pans, or the equivalent in ovensafe dishes. Arrange a pretty pattern of garnishy stuff in the bottom of each, then pour a little of the cooled stock over them. Chill until set, then arrange the meat carefully on top, topping up with as much of the stock as it takes to cover the meat. Put the *zalatina* back in the fridge to set: once it is quite firm, you can use a hot palette knife to ease it out of the molds and turn it out so that the garnish is uppermost. Serve in thick slices with plenty of bread and pickled vegetables or lemon.

Kubba Halabi

RICE *KIBBEH*

I was really pleased when I discovered that not all traditional *kibbeh/kubba* are made with wheat. This (mostly) Iraqi recipe features a mashed-up rice casing, with a wholesome and unusual filling. Other non-wheat *kibbeh* use mashed potato, corn, or ground rice: the truth is of course that you could write a book just about *kibbeh*. If you were very patient… *kibbeh* are nothing if not fiddly. Which is probably why they are such popular street fare, for, while all Arabic housewives have a signature recipe for this dish, there is nothing quite like having someone else make them for you.

MAKES ABOUT 10

FOR THE FILLING:
3 scallions, finely chopped
oil, for frying
10½ oz/300g ground lamb
1 heaped tsp *baharat* (or a cheaters mixture of
    black pepper, paprika, cumin, and coriander)
1 level tsp lime powder or add the zest of
    1 lime (it won't be the same but it will help)
1¾ oz/50g raisins (soaked for 10 minutes)
1¾ oz/50g chopped nuts (you choose which)

big handful of fresh parsley, chopped
salt

FOR THE CASING:
¾ cup/5½oz/150g split red lentils
2 cups/14oz/400g short-grain rice
1 level tsp ground turmeric
½ tsp salt
5½ oz/150g halloumi or mozzarella, grated
    (optional but scrummy)
rice flour as required (actually any flour will
    do, but let's keep it all gluten-free, shall we?)

Fry the onions in a little oil. After a couple of minutes, add the lamb, stirring well, followed by the spices. When the lamb is just starting to brown, mix in the (drained) raisins, mixed nuts, and parsley, together with salt to taste, and set aside to cool a little.

Meanwhile, boil the lentils with the rice until the latter is slightly overcooked, adding the turmeric towards the end of the cooking time. Drain, then stir the salt and grated cheese through the rice, mashing and pummeling it all so that it coheres into one sticky ball (if you have a food processor with a meat-grinding function, this would do the job very well). Using wet hands, break off a lump the size of a large egg and mold it into an oval shape. Cup this egg-shaped lump in one hand and use your forefinger to poke a cavity in the *kibbeh*. Next, insert a teaspoonful of the lamb mixture and then use your thumb and finger to pinch the rice mix together so that the filling is completely encased. Repeat with the rest of the rice paste.

Spread a little rice flour out on a tray and roll the *kibbeh* very gently in it before arranging on a tray and chilling for an hour or so. Deep-fry the *kibbeh* in hot oil (in batches if necessary) until they are golden brown, then remove them carefully and drain them on paper towel. Serve hot with lemon wedges.

Kufteh Tabrizi
FANCY-ISH STUFFED MEATBALLS

There is a town called Tabriz in Iran that is renowned for crafting *kufteh*. Their most famous recipe contains a whole poussin (baby chicken). This recipe is slightly less ostentatious, and undeniably far more piquant and intriguing.

MEZZE FOR 8

FOR THE STOCK:

1 large onion, chopped

oil, for frying

½ very hot red chili (or 2 green chilies), chopped (optional)

1 red bell pepper, finely chopped

1 tsp ground turmeric

1 tbsp tomato paste

1 can (14oz/400g) chopped tomatoes

¾ cup/200ml sour grape juice (or just add extra stock and the juice of 2 lemons)

8 cups/2 liters good chicken stock

salt and freshly ground black pepper

FOR THE CASING:

½ cup/3½oz/100g yellow split peas (chana dal)

½ cup/3½oz/100g short-grain rice

1lb 10oz/750g ground lamb

1 large onion, grated

1 tsp ground turmeric

1 tsp dried oregano

1 tsp dried tarragon

1 level tsp salt

½ tsp ground black pepper

FOR THE STUFFING:

3½ oz/100g barberries, soaked (or cranberries)

scant ½ cup/2¾oz/75g pitted prunes, soaked

scant ½ cup/2¾oz/75g dried apricots or peaches, soaked

generous 5 tbsp/2¾oz/75g butter

¾ cup/2¾oz/75g walnuts, roughly chopped

½ cup/2¾oz/75g chopped nuts (almonds and pistachios)

1¾oz/50g sour or morello cherries, pitted

scant 1⅓ cups/5½oz/150g breadcrumbs

1 tsp ground cinnamon

½ tsp ground cardamom

1 tbsp tomato paste

First the stock: you'll need a large pan. Fry the onion in a little oil. After a minute or so, add the chili and red pepper, followed after a few minutes by the turmeric, tomato paste and chopped tomatoes, sour grape juice, and stock. Bring to a boil, season, cover, and set aside.

Next, the casing. Cook the split peas in boiling water until soft, around 35 minutes, and do the same for the rice, around 15 minutes. Drain both and cool before adding to the lamb, along with the onion, turmeric, herbs, and seasoning. Pound the mixture well: you can actually start it off in a blender unless you are game for the exercise. Chill until ready.

Finally, the stuffing. Drain the soaked fruit and pat it dry. Roughly chop the prunes and apricots/peaches. Melt the butter and fry all the fruit and nuts together, stirring well, for 6–7 minutes. Add the remaining ingredients, cook a little more, then take off the heat.

To cook the *kufteh*, bring the stock back to a boil. Use wet hands to form the meat mixture into 8 large balls. Form a hollow in each one, and divide the stuffing mixture between them, closing the casing up over the filling. Drop the meatballs into the bubbling stock, cover the pan, and cook for 1 hour, or until the *kufteh* have risen to the top of the stock. Serve covered with the tomato stock as hot *mezze*—or cool and offer them up as a very refined picnic dish.

Lahana Dolma

TURKISH STUFFED CABBAGE LEAVES WITH BONUS GREEK SAUCE

MAKES AROUND 24

1 medium green or white cabbage
    (about 3lb 5oz/1.5kg)

14oz/400g ground lamb

½ cup/3½ oz/100g long-grain
    rice (I use basmati)

1 onion, very finely chopped

2 tbsp raisins, soaked for
    20 minutes and drained

2 tbsp pine nuts or sunflower
    seed kernels

big handful of fresh parsley,
    chopped

1 tbsp dried dill

salt and freshly ground
    black pepper

slosh of olive oil

2 tbsp grape *pekmez* (optional)

FOR THE SAUCE*:

1½ tsp cornstarch

2 eggs, separated

juice of 1 lemon

* Handy hint

This classic *avgolemono* (egg
and lemon sauce) can be used
with all sorts of things from
asparagus to fish to meatballs.
Just so you know.

Most Middle Eastern countries stuff things, and all lay claim to inventing the idea/making the best *dolma*. Thanks to the Ottoman kitchens, the Turks field an impressive array of filled vegetables, and when it comes to cabbage leaves, they are most certainly in the lead. But in the interests of international relations, I have added some Greek sauce to the matter.

Discard any mangy looking outer leaves from the cabbage, and carefully remove and wash the rest of the leaves, one by one. Bring a large pan of salted water to a boil and blanch the leaves in batches for around 2 minutes (for green cabbage) or 3½ minutes (for white) before draining them in a colander.

Mix the minced lamb with the rice, onion, raisins, pine nuts, herbs, and seasoning. Take about 2 teaspoonfuls of the stuffing and place it at the stalk end of one of the cabbage leaves. Next, roll the cabbage leaf away from you, over the stuffing, tucking in the bits at the side as you go: you should end up with a small sausage shape, with the rice/meat mix completely enclosed. Repeat with the rest of the mixture, keeping any damaged leaves to one side. Place an upturned plate in the base of a saucepan, and cover it with those reject leaves before arranging the rolled *dolmeh* concentrically in the pan and adding the olive oil and *pekmez*, if using. Place another plate on top of the cabbage leaves, then fill the pan with water so that the leaves are just covered. Bring to a boil, cover, turn down the heat, and simmer gently for about 1 hour, then take off the heat.

Remove the lid of the pan to let some of the steam out, then carefully tip the pan over a small saucepan, pressing the plate on top down to keep the *dolmeh* in place, so that any remaining cooking stock trickles out. Keep the *dolmeh* warm while you make the egg and lemon sauce.

Top up the *dolmeh* stock to around a generous ¾ cup/200ml by adding boiling water if necessary, then pour a little of it into a little bowl, adding the cornstarch and mixing well. Add a little more stock, stir, and pour all of the cornstarch mixture back into the pan with the rest of the stock in it. Whisk the egg whites until stiff-ish, then beat in the egg yolks and lemon juice, followed, a little at a time, by the stock. Pour it all back into the pan and heat gently for a few minutes, without boiling.

Arrange the *lahana dolma* on a plate, drizzle the sauce over the top, and serve hot or warm.

COOKING WITH LEFTOVERS

Of course, some of the most satisfying snacks comprise leftovers: they sate both one's hunger and one's wallet. This is a double posting of two of our favorite things to do with the rest of a roast dinner. I have been vague about quantities, because, frankly, I have no idea how much meat you have left over. These are both throw-it-in-the-dish-and-be-done-with-measuring-type recipes.

SHREDDED LAMB WITH CROÛTONS

There are folks who think that the best thing about roast lamb is its by-products: dripping, shepherd's pie, bone marrow… Know what, I'm drooling as I type this. I am not that partial to meat, and avoided lamb altogether until I became exposed to the Middle Eastern treatment, but now there are nights when nothing else will do.

Fry 2 of the garlic cloves in plenty of oil before adding the bread cubes, stirring well, followed by the thyme. Cook for 2 minutes, then drain on a piece of paper towel.

Heat a little more oil in the pan and fry the onion. When it starts to color, add the rest of the garlic together with the lamb and fenugreek and cook for 2–3 minutes. Season, add the lemon juice, and simmer for a few minutes more before stirring the green stuff through the dish. Toss the croûtons on top and serve.

SERVES 2–4
5 garlic cloves, minced
non-extra-virgin olive oil
a few slices of stale bread, cut
    into ½ in/1 cm cubes
1 tsp dried thyme
1 small onion, chopped
1–2 cups of leftover cooked
    lamb, shredded
1–2 tsp dried fenugreek leaves
salt and ground black pepper
1–2 tbsp lemon juice
big handful/s of fresh green stuff:
    spinach, chives, cilantro,
    parsley, watercress

CHICKEN WITH OKRA

You shouldn't really need pointers as to what to do with leftover chicken: it is one of the most versatile foodstuffs in the world. But here's our piastre's worth anyway.

Fry the onion in a little oil. Once it softens, add the garlic, stirring well, followed by the okra. When the latter start to brown, add the chicken and tomatoes, followed by the lime juice and pickle. Cover the pan and simmer for 7–8 minutes before seasoning to taste, sprinkling with chopped herbs and serving with warm bread.

SERVES 2–4
1 medium onion, chopped
oil, for frying
2–3 garlic cloves, chopped
1lb 2oz/500g baby okra (ladies'
    fingers), washed and dried
1–2 cups of leftover cooked
    chicken, cut into chunks
10½ oz/300g cherry tomatoes
juice of 1 lime
2 tbsp mango pickle
salt to taste (may be unnecessary
    as the pickle will be salty)
big handful of fresh cilantro
    and/or mint, washed and
    chopped

Hot Vegetarian Mezze

Mullah Nasruddin was flattered to find himself on the guest list for a meal at the palace one evening, and even more so when he learned he was to sit at the head table.

The first course was a specially created dish of spinach stewed with pekmez. The King, valuing the wise man's opinion, asked Nasruddin what he thought of it.

"Fabulous!" cried the Mullah. "'Loved every mouthful!"

"That's interesting," replied the King, "I thought it was really dire."

"Well, yes, actually I agree," said Nasruddin. "It wasn't good."

The King looked puzzled. "Hold on: a minute ago you said you liked it..."

"Well it's like this, your majesty," the Mullah answered, unperturbed, "As it happens, I live in and serve the realm of the King, not the Kingdom of the Stewed Spinach."

Of course, if you are a guest in someone's home it is only polite to tell them what they want to hear—and (national and international "disturbances" in the Middle East notwithstanding) Snackistanis are nothing if not diplomatic.

But hopefully this tale serves to highlight what I am trying to achieve in this chapter, which is to show off some of the region's most sensational, if unusual, vegetable combos. Ingredients are prepared in a way that is utterly different from our usual treatment of them. Basic materials that you might have in your fridge are turned into tasty snacks, comforting suppers, and mezze dishes. Sweet and savory, sweet and sour, heavily herby, sensationally spiced fare packed full of contrast and surprise, stuff that will get your guests talking or your family clamoring for more. Because meat and fish have enjoyed prominence for far too long.

IRANIAN STREET VEGGIES

The heart of most Iranian towns is the bazaar—some, like Tehran and Isfahan, are truly vast, dense, and often mysterious rambling mazes, a town within a town. And it is here that there is the greatest need for street food—simple snacks to nourish weary shoppers or fortify traders. Street snacks in Iran are nothing if not simple, but it is this very simplicity that intrigues me, and I have learned to take a fresh look at some of the ingredients they use and treat them with great respect. Favorites in the winter months are boiled turnips or beets; a perennial feature are the hot potato vendors; in the spring there are fava beans; and in the summer you can buy grilled corn. Of course, such food never tastes as good as it does when eaten *in situ*, whether it be in the bitter cold or sweltering heat, out of newspaper or wax paper cones, but I have tried to recreate some of these simple pleasures…

SHALGAM—TURNIPS

If possible, buy young, baby turnips—big old wrinklies belong to the stockpot or stew. Scrub the skins of each turnip well, then quarter them. Although the skins are not eaten, leaving them on during cooking ensures that the vegetables remain intact. Place in a pan, cover with water, and bring to a boil. Do not salt the water, as this makes the turnips tough and they will take longer to cook. Turn down the heat and simmer for around 45 minutes, or until a fork prods into them with ease. Drain and serve with salt and pepper. They are absolutely delicious. But if you're still not convinced, try mashing them with a little butter and a grating of nutmeg. Or you could check out the Iraqi recipe on p.114.

LABOO—BEET

To cook beets bazaari-style, just peel and cut them into manageable chunks. Cover with water (again, no salt), bring to a boil, then turn down the heat and simmer for 1½ hours. Convention will have you add around 2 teaspoons sugar per 2 lb 4oz/1kg of beets—this is a matter of taste, and I find most people make them too sweet. Just enjoy with a fork. It's not remotely authentic, but I like them with a big dollop of mascarpone on the side.

STREET CORN

Again, a very simple idea. As someone who grew up eating corn smothered in butter, this method of preparation came as something of a revelation. Grill your corn cobs in their husks over fire, shuck them, then plunge into hot salted water for a few moments. Eat. Told you it was simple. I never thought that I would find butter superfluous to my requirements…

BOGOLI—BROAD BEANS

For *bazaari bogoli* (4 people can easily eat 4lb 8oz–6lb 8oz/2–3kg of whole fava/broad beans—by the time they are shelled they don't go very far), bring a large pan of water to a boil (again, no salt until later), and plunge them into the boiling water. Turn down the heat and simmer for around 45 minutes to 1 hour. Drain and serve still in their pods accompanied by salt, a pot of *golpar* (see p.10), and lemon wedges. Iranians invariably shuck their beans; personally, I prefer to eat them with the skin on.

BABY EGGPLANT *DOLMEH*

This is a recipe from our refrigerator aisle. It's really kind of Mother Nature to design stuff in snack-sized portions as well as its regular size. Baby eggplants are perfect for snacking on, and these *dolmeh* (which are kind of like mini *Imam Biyaldi*) make a wonderful *mezze* dish.

You can use white or purple varieties: the white ones are usually chunkier and need a bit more cooking—although having said that, they are often eaten raw and are not unpleasant *al dente*.

MAKES 8

8 baby eggplants
salt
1 small red onion, roughly sliced
2 garlic cloves, sliced
16 shelled walnut quarters

8 pitted dates, halved
1½ tbsp grape *pekmez*
    (or pomegranate molasses)
4 tbsp tomato concasse (or juice)
½ tsp red pepper flakes
1 tbsp olive oil

Make a lengthways incision in each of the eggplants, taking care not to pierce right through. Sprinkle a little salt into each of the cavities, and rub it in before inverting the vegetables onto paper towels to drain for 30 minutes.

Preheat the oven to 375°F/190°C.

Wipe the eggplants to remove any residual bitterness/water/salt. Insert a chunk of onion and a couple of slices of garlic into each cavity, then press a couple of pieces of walnut and date into each. Layer them into an ovensafe dish.

Whisk all of the other ingredients together and drizzle the resulting sauce over the eggplants. Cover the dish and bake for around 40 minutes, or until the eggplant flesh is soft when you poke it.

Enjoy while still warm: these make a great *mezze* item, or a fancy addition to your picnic.

Kabak Kizartmasi
TURKISH ZUCCHINI FRITTERS WITH YOGURT "SAUCE"

You can practically coat anything in batter and fry it and you will get a line of salivating people at your kitchen door. Obviously this is not everyday food (because we are all watching our fat intake, yes?), but it is a simple snack option and makes for a great little *mezze* dish.

The Turks seem partial to vegetables thus prepared and there is a whole range of *kizartmasi* dishes: eggplants, carrots, cauliflower, and potato all get the same treatment. But zucchinis, with their refined bitterness, lend themselves particularly well to the creamy crunchiness of batter.

MEZZE FOR 4

generous 1 cup/5½ oz/150g all-purpose flour

½ tsp salt

½ tsp ground black pepper

½ cup/125ml beer (yes, you may drink the rest: it'd be a shame to waste it)

1 level tsp ground turmeric

1 level tsp paprika

2 large zucchini, cut into
⅛–⅙ in/3–4mm slices

oil, for frying

TO SERVE:

scant ½ cup/3½ oz/100g plain, not too thick yogurt

4 garlic cloves, minced

pinch of salt

drizzle of olive oil

squeeze of lemon

Aleppo pepper (or a mix of cayenne and paprika)

Sift a scant ¾ cup/3½oz/100g of the flour into a bowl along with the salt and pepper, then slowly whisk in the beer until you get a smooth, thick batter. Set the bowl aside for about 1 hour so that the batter can "rest."

Scatter the rest of the flour on a plate and mix in the turmeric and paprika. Dip the zucchini slices in and out of the flour. Heat a good glug of oil in a frying pan and give the rested beer batter a good stir. Take one of the floured zucchini slices and dunk it into the batter; allow to drain, then fry in the hot oil, turning after 2 minutes, until it is golden on both sides. Repeat with the rest of the zucchini slices: you will probably have to cook them in two batches.

Mix the yogurt with the garlic, adding salt, olive oil, and lemon to taste. Sprinkle the *kizartmasi* with the Aleppo pepper, and serve them on a plate with the garlic sauce in a bowl on the side.

THREE-PEA "TAGINE"

As tagines go, this is a cinch, and it is very easy on the eye, since practically all the ingredients are spherical. It is a quick dish to prepare, and so if you are lucky enough to own a tagine dish, you can either use it as a serving dish, or transfer all the ingredients into your tagine at the same time as you add the green peas: put it in the oven at 300°F/150°C for around 30 minutes, or until you want to serve.

The addition of warm "dunky" bread makes it a great informal supper dish, or you could cook less and dish it up as part of a *mezze* spread.

MOROCCAN TV DINNER FOR 4

14oz/400g can chickpeas, drained
   (or ½ cup/3½ oz/100g dried chickpeas,
   soaked overnight)
1 cup/7oz/200g yellow split peas (chana dal)
½ cup/2¾ oz/75g raisins
1 large onion, chopped
olive oil, for frying
3 garlic cloves, minced
1 level tsp ground ginger
1 tsp ground turmeric
1 level tsp ground cumin

1 tsp ground cinnamon
½ tsp red pepper flakes (optional)
scant 2½ cups/550ml vegetable stock
   (or water)
3 cups/12oz/350g frozen peas (or fresh if it is
   that time of year)
around 12 cherry tomatoes
salt and freshly ground black pepper
½ bunch of fresh cilantro, chopped
½ bunch of fresh mint, shredded

If you are using dried chickpeas, rinse them and cook in fresh water for about 1½ hours, or until they are soft without falling apart: the addition of a pinch of baking soda will accelerate the cooking process.

Soak the split peas for around 45 minutes. Likewise, the raisins, although they only need 20 minutes' soaking time.

Fry the onion in a little oil, then once it has softened and become translucent, add the garlic and spices and cook for 2 minutes, stirring constantly. Add the stock or water and bring to a boil before lowering in the drained split peas, turning the heat down and leaving to simmer (you may need to top up the cooking liquid during this time).

After about 45 minutes, drain the raisins and add them to the tagine, together with the cooked/canned chickpeas, frozen peas, cherry tomatoes, and a little salt and pepper. Bubble away for a further 10 minutes, or until the peas and tomatoes are cooked. Take the pan/tagine off the heat or out of the oven, check and adjust the seasoning, and finally sprinkle the contents liberally with the chopped herbs. Enjoy hot or just warm.

Perfect for a Sunday evening in front of the TV, watching *Casablanca* of course.

Esfanaj va Rivas
SPINACH WITH RHUBARB AND POMEGRANATE

I frequently put together something like this for my lunch. It is a well-known fact that shopkeepers are tied to their registers on very long pieces of elastic, and always have to be "back in five minutes." Stir-fries like this are therefore a boon: they take little more than five minutes to prepare, and are certainly healthier than going down to the fish and chip shop.

This recipe is based on one of my favorite Persian *khoreshts* or casseroles: the original dish comprises chicken, which I don't really like and which clearly takes a little longer to cook.

SNACK LUNCH FOR
1 HUNGRY SHOPKEEPER
2–3 scallions, chopped
sunflower (or other) oil, for cooking
½ tsp ground turmeric
1 garlic clove, chopped
big handful of parsley, roughly chopped
big handful of mint, roughly chopped
1 glass water (about ⅔ cup/150ml)
½ can (7oz/200g) chickpeas, drained
2–3 sticks of rhubarb, peeled (if large, mature
    stalks) and cut into 1¼in/3cm chunks

1 tsp sugar
½ bunch of spinach, roughly shredded
juice of ½ a lemon
1 tbsp pomegranate molasses (or *pekmez*,
    or just add extra lemon)
salt and freshly ground black pepper
    and sugar if required
fresh pomegranate, to garnish (optional:
    pomegranates are a winter fruit, while
    rhubarb is at its best in early summer)

Fry the onions in a splash of oil. Once they have softened, add the turmeric and garlic followed by the herbs. Cook for about 5 minutes, stirring well, before adding the water. Bring the contents of the pan to a boil, then add the chickpeas, rhubarb, and sugar. Simmer for around 5 minutes before adding the spinach, lemon juice, and pomegranate molasses. Bubble for 5 minutes more, season to taste, and serve with warm bread. Scowl at the customers knocking on the door and indicate that they should form an orderly line until you have finished your lunch...

This combo is famously "cold" (*sard*) in Persian dietetics—only the mint and the chickpeas are "warm" (*garm*). Iranians to this day believe that you are what you eat, and that all food has hot or cold properties that serve to slow down or accelerate your metabolism. Too much cold food leaves you feeling bilious and out of sorts; too much hot food can leave you restless and febrile. By way of example, alcohol is very "cold," which is why so many hangover cures comprise "hot" (heavy, greasy) foods. So now you know.

Qorma-e-Piaz

AFGHAN SWEET-AND-SOUR ONION HOTPOT

* Ajwain seeds

These are also known as carom seeds or bishop's weed. They are highly aromatic and used mostly as a home remedy in Afghanistan: they are chewed to sweeten the breath, and made into a decoction for all manner of digestive ills. In food they are used sparingly: the flavor is somewhere between aniseed and thyme, but very strong. In most recipes, they can be replaced by cumin seeds.

** Pine nuts (jalghouz)

These are big (in size) in Afghanistan and very popular. They are most frequently enjoyed roasted in their skins, in much the same way as pistachios. Most Snackistani recipes involving pine nuts have their origins in the Levant and Turkey: they get into *kibbeh*, puddings, rice, stuffing… There are two problems with them: one is that they are fiendishly expensive, and quite often in short supply. The other is that the Chinese variety can cause a nasty reaction known as Pine Mouth: it is harmless but deeply unpleasant, as it results in everything tasting metallic or bitter for days (for more about this, see the Veggiestan website). Pumpkin and sunflower seed kernels make admirable alternatives, and are both a lot cheaper and healthier.

This is an unusual recipe. I've always thought that it takes a brave cook to create a dish without onions in it: turns out it feels just as weird placing the onions center stage. *Qorma* is a generic Afghan term used for food cooked in a sauce that has been thickened with vegetables or legumes or nuts—in other words, a fat, satisfying, pleasingly oily stew.

SIMPLE SUPPER FOR 4

½ cup/3½ oz/100g yellow split peas (chana dal)
½ cup/2¾ oz/75g raisins
oil, for frying
½ tsp ajwain (or use caraway seeds)*
1 tsp mustard seeds
2 garlic cloves, minced
1 large onion, diced
1 red bell pepper, diced
2 green chilies, chopped
½ in/1 cm stub fresh ginger
½ tsp ground turmeric
1 tsp garam masala
around 20 (small) shallots, peeled but left whole
2 tsp tomato paste
2 tbsp vinegar
salt, to taste
generous ⅓ cup/1¾ oz/50g pine nuts**

Pick through the the split peas and soak them in cold water for around 45 minutes. The raisins also need soaking, for about 15 minutes.

Heat a good glug of oil in a decent-sized (and fairly deep) frying pan. Once it is sizzling hot, toss in the ajwain and mustard seeds, stirring constantly, followed by the garlic. Cook for less than a minute, then scoop them out of the oil with a slotted spoon and set aside. Once the oil is hot again, tip in the onion, pepper, chili, and ginger and cook until the onion has softened. Add the spices, followed a few moments later by the shallots. Cook until they have started to brown, and then stir in the tomato paste and vinegar.

Drain the split peas and raisins, and add them to the pan together with just enough water to cover everything. Set to simmer: the *qorma* will need about 50 minutes to cook through. Just before you want to serve and eat, season the dish to taste before stirring the reserved fried seeds and garlic back into the pan. Finally, dry-fry the pine nuts until they start to color.

Serve the *qorma* garnished with the toasted pine nuts; warm flatbread and some nice thick yogurt make fitting accompaniments.

LETTUCE *KOOKOO*

Kookoo (great name, no?) are basically Persian omelettes. They can be made as individual patties, or as a regular, circular, pan-sized job. And they come in a huge range of flavors, from sugary through to sour. The most famous type is *kookoo-ye-sabzi*, which is a lush herby snack, often studded with barberries and walnuts. But more recently my *kookoo* of choice has been this one. This is for several reasons: firstly, I always experience a shiver of culinary excitement when I cook with lettuce. I mean, it's a salad vegetable: cooking with it just seems so *avant garde*; secondly, it is a handy way to use up sad, soggy neglected leaves; and thirdly, it is so easy to make.

SERVES 6 AS A SNACK

oil, for frying (canola is a healthy option and is growing in popularity across the Middle East)

3–4 scallions, diced

12 eggs

2 tsp all-purpose flour

¼ tsp baking soda

½ medium iceberg lettuce, cross shredded (but not too finely)

salt and freshly ground black pepper

Heat a dash of oil in a frying pan and sizzle the scallions until they have softened. Take off the heat and drain on paper towel.

Break the eggs into a bowl and whisk well before beating in the flour and baking soda. Add the lettuce and the cooled scallions to the mix, together with 1 level teaspoon of salt and a healthy sprinkle of pepper.

Heat some more oil in the frying pan: you need it to be just-before-smoking hot. Using a tablespoon, dollop the eggy mixture into the oil in rough, flat oval shapes, allowing them to cook for 2 minutes before turning them over with a spatula. When the *kookoo* are golden brown on both sides, scoop them on to paper towel to drain. Repeat until you have cooked all of the mixture.

Serve hot or cold wrapped in flatbread of your choice; pickled veggies and fresh herbs would be nice but optional extras.

If lettuce feels like a Western thing

Let's face it, our salads invariably consist mostly of the stuff, whereas it seldom dominates in Middle Eastern salad bowls. It has in fact been enjoyed across Snackistan for thousands of years, chiefly thanks to the Egyptians' discovery that eating lots of it can make you rather frisky (although, confusingly, the ancient Greeks later worked out that if you eat just a little it is quite soporific): this is because it contains stimulating tropane alkaloids (a bit like the nightshade family), but I will refrain from getting any more technical as we are meant to be cooking rather than discoursing ethnobotany.

Beid Baghdadi
SPECIAL BAGHDADI EGGS

When it comes to the human diet, the egg most certainly came before the chicken—we've been snacking on them practically from the moment we slithered out of the sea (or whatever). They are referred to in ancient Mesopotamian texts, represented in Egyptian hieroglyphs, and much fêted by the Romans (who ate them with nearly every meal, hence the expression "from the egg to the apple"). And there are quite a few recipes for them in Al-Baghdadi's thirteenth-century *oeuvre*: here, for your culinary pleasure, are the two most user-friendly recipes from that tome (i.e., the ones that don't call for sheep tail fat, rancid barley, and blood…).

BAID MUTAJJAN AKA FRIED EGGS

For when you've got that morning-after-the-epoch-before kind of feeling…

Heat a good slosh of oil in a frying pan and crack the eggs in. As they start to set, sprinkle them with the spices followed by the soy sauce. Serve with warm bread. Medieval costumes optional.

MEDIEVAL BRUNCH
FOR 2–4
sesame oil, for cooking
4 large free-range eggs
¼ tsp ground cinnamon
¼ tsp ground cumin
¼ tsp ground coriander
½ tsp soy sauce

BAID MAKHSOUS AKA SPECIAL EGGS

I first came across this recipe in an art installation by the rather wonderful Jake Tilson. His culinary derring-do sent me skedaddling off to find the original *Kitab al-Tabih*: it is a recommended tome for those with an interest in Middle Eastern food history, and Charles Perry's translation is very accessible.

Heat a dash of sesame oil in a frying pan and toss in the celery and caraway seeds. Once the celery has softened, add the other spices, stirring well, then add the vinegar. Bring to a boil, season to taste, and crack the eggs carefully on top. Cover the pan and fry/steam until the eggs are set. Sprinkle with paprika (an inauthentic extra) and serve (preferably from the pan—eggs are always better out of the pan) with warm bread. Share with your favorite vizier.

MEDIEVAL BRUNCH
FOR 2–4
sesame oil, for cooking
3–4 sticks of celery, chopped
½ tsp caraway seeds
¼ tsp ground cinnamon
½ tsp ground coriander
¼ tsp ground saffron dissolved
    in a splash of boiling water
4 tbsp red wine vinegar
salt and coarsely ground
    black pepper
4 large free-range eggs
paprika, to garnish

Saganaki
FLAMING CHEESE

Mmmmm. Fried cheese. Halloumi is not the only hot turophilian delight to emerge from the lands abutting the Aegean: the Greeks have a penchant for frying all kinds of cheese, and it is a hugely popular *mezze* dish. The word *saganaki* refers not only to the offering of fried cheese, but also to the dish in which it is served: a small, two-handled sizzler tray, a little like an Indian tandoor. Seafood and some vegetables can also be prepared and served in a *saganaki*.

You can just flour and fry the cheese, but this flambé version lends a little theater to the dish—and food is always better with added theater.

Dip the cheese slices either in water or milk and allow to drain for a few seconds before coating each slice with flour. Melt the butter in your *saganaki* dish (a frying pan is just fine), adding a glug of oil to stop the butter burning. Once it is sizzle hot, fry the coated cheese for 2 minutes per side, or until it just begins to assume an appetizing golden color.

If you are showing off, now is the time to assemble your guests. Hold the spoonful of ouzo over the pan, and touch a flame to its surface. Tip it over the cheese and shake the pan, thus eliciting "oohs" and "aahs" from your (apparently easily impressed) audience. Sprinkle with plenty of black pepper, garnish with the lemon wedges, and serve immediately.

SNACKETTE FOR 4

8 thick (½ in/1 cm at least) slices cheese: ideally a hard Greek cheese such as *kefalotyri*, halloumi, or *kasseri*, but mozzarella or mild cheddar work well too

water or milk, for dipping

flour, for coating

3½ tbsp/1¾ oz/50g butter

oil, for frying (olive is best here)

1 tbsp ouzo (or brandy)

freshly ground black pepper

1 lemon, cut into wedges

FRIED WATERMELON WITH HALLOUMI

We got really excited when we first realized that you can fry watermelon. It feels kind of wrong, wayward, wacky—and everyone needs to be wrong, wayward, and wacky in the kitchen sometimes. Watermelon has always been a perfect foil for cheese, and no time is a bad time for halloumi, and so we thought we'd just try sizzling them together. Lo—a new snack addiction was born.

Sprinkle both sides of each slice of watermelon with the spice mix. Pour enough oil into a frying pan so as just to cover the bottom, and heat it to sizzling point. Fry the watermelon; once it is hot all the way through, remove the slices to a plate. Now fry the halloumi quickly on each side: it should be golden but not dark brown. Spread the halloumi on a platter, arrange the watermelon on top, and sprinkle the whole thing with mint. Don't burn your mouth as you scarf it.

SERVES 6 AS A REAL SIMPLE *MEZZE* DISH

12–15 "triangular" slices (⅜ in thick/7–8mm) of watermelon, skinned

2–3 tsp Snackistan Patent Harissa Spice Mix (see p.21)

olive oil, for frying

1 pack (8oz/225g) halloumi, cut into 12–15 slices (⅛ in/3mm thick)

big handful of fresh mint, shredded

IFTAR: BEST SNACK OF THE DAY

Iftar, or "breakfast." We're not talking any old cornflake breakfast, but the first food and drink of the day for those who have fasted. During the month of Ramadan, and on and off throughout the year, Muslims abstain from food, drink, and smoking during the hours between sunrise and sunset, as proscribed in the Koran. It is thought that this teaches the body discipline, and helps the believer focus on more esoteric matters. *Iftar* is the name given to the food used to break fast: this could take place at 4pm during the short days of winter months, or as late as 11pm during the long days of summer (the Islamic year follows the lunar calendar, and so the months "move back" around 10 days each year if you offset them against the Gregorian calendar).

Iftar is rarely a full meal, but usually comprises a snack or a series of snacks, which are consumed prior to a proper evening meal. For most Muslims the first thing that passes their lips is dates: again, this is specified in the Koran:

"Whoever finds dates should break his fast with them and the one who does not should break his fast with water because it is pure."

Dates have been recognized as a snacking "super-food" for millennia: they have long been used to restore weary desert travelers, but modern nutritionists think they are as close to being "the perfect food" as we are likely to find, as they are packed full of minerals, vitamins, and natural sugar. They are, as one of our own suppliers proudly boasts, "energetic fruits for sportsmen especially engaged in sporting activities." Hurrah for mistranslations the world over.

Having supped on dates and water, the hungry fast-breaker will move on to sweet tea, bread, cheese, and eggs. Clearly Snackistan is quite a big place, and favored *iftar* foods vary from village to village, country to country, but the essence of the repast is the same. Families, neighbors, congregations gather together to eat. My own family-in-law eat dishes such as *cotelettes* (meat patties) with flatbread, *fereni* (a sweet custard-like pudding made with rice flour) or *halim* (porridge made with chicken, see p.74) or *sholeh zard* (saffron rice pudding), *kookoo* (omelettes—see p.108), hard-boiled eggs, *dolmeh*, and lots and lots of fruit. They also quite like my fried watermelon (see p.111). Quite often my mother-in-law (and fasting housewives the Muslim world over) will spend five or six hours carefully crafting these foods.

Dinner is served a few hours later, and many will also get up to pray and eat just before dawn (in a snack known as *sahar*), the better to fortify themselves for the long abstemious day ahead.

Chakchouka
TUNISIAN EGGS WITH ATTITUDE

Of recipes for scrambled eggs incorporating vegetables, herbs, and spices there are aplenty, but this offering from North Africa ramps up the spice quotient and leaves the eggs perfectly poached and whole. This is perfect Sunday brunch fare—it will certainly enliven your breakfast table conversation—but it makes a good snack any time. Feel free to add some spicy chopped *merguez* sausages.

Cook the onion and pepper in a generous quantity of olive oil. When they soften, add the zucchini and garlic, stirring well. After a few minutes, add the cumin and tomatoes, followed by the tomato and harissa paste. Next pour in the tomato juice, season to taste, and bring the contents of the pan to a gentle simmer.

Make 4 small "wells" in the vegetable mixture, crack an egg into each, then cover the pan. Cook until the eggs are set, around 10 minutes, and sprinkle with parsley. Serve straight from the pan (your guests will think you're being quaintly ethnic, when in fact the gesture is an effort to reduce the morning-after-the-night-before dish washing), with warm bread.

SERVES 4

1 medium onion, chopped
1 green bell pepper, chopped
good olive oil, for cooking
1 zucchini, diced
2 garlic cloves, minced
½ tsp ground cumin
4 large tomatoes, cut into chunks
2 tsp tomato paste
2 tsp harissa paste
scant ½ cup/100ml tomato juice
    (or water)
salt to taste
4 large free-range eggs
big handful of fresh parsley,
    chopped

CARROTS COOKED IN *PEKMEZ*

Carrots are such humble, obliging vegetables: it is nice to give them their own little dish in which to star. The Moroccans make much of them in salad, but this recipe owes more to Turkey and Iran, whence the vegetable in all likelihood originated. Early, wild species of Asian carrots were magenta in color, so these fancy-colored jobs you see in supermarkets are in fact nothing new.

Blanch the carrots in boiling water for 2 minutes, adding the orange peel to the boiling water for the last 30 seconds. Drain the contents of the pan, reserving about scant ¼ cup/50ml of the water.

Melt the butter in a frying pan and add the carrots, orange, and ginger. When the carrots start to brown, tip the *pekmez* and orange blossom water into the pan along with the reserved cooking water, stirring well, then add the brown sugar. Bubble for a few minutes, season, and serve sprinkled with the chopped nuts.

MEZZE OR SIDE FOR 4

1lb 2oz/500g carrots, peeled and
    cut into chunky sticks (unless
    very thin, in which case halve
    them or cook whole)
1oz/25g dried sour orange peel
    (or pare the skin from a fresh
    orange and cut it into very
    thin strips)
7 tbsp/3½ oz/100g salted butter
½ in/1cm piece fresh ginger,
    peeled and minced
scant ¼ cup/50ml
    grape *pekmez* (or use
    pomegranate molasses)
1 tsp orange blossom water
2 tsp brown sugar
salt and ground black pepper
⅓ cup/1¾ oz/50g chopped
    pistachios (or almonds)

Shahan Fouls
SUDANESE MASHED FAVA BEANS

BREAKFAST FOR 4

scant 1¾ cups/10½ oz/300g
    whole dried fava (broad)
    beans, soaked overnight
pinch of baking soda
2 tbsp unroasted sesame oil
salt
1 tsp ground cumin
½ tsp ground fenugreek seeds
3½ oz/100g white (feta-style)
    cheese, crumbled
4 eggs
oil, for frying
2 large tomatoes, cut into chunks
1 small onion, cut into chunks
1 green bell pepper, chopped
2–3 green chilies, chopped

Sudan is an honorary member of the Snackistan Republic on account of its proximity to the Arabian peninsula: its culture and cuisine have a lot in common with the rest of the Middle East. And they make excellent *fouls medammes*. As with other Snackistani nations, this is a popular breakfast/street dish. You know, I could write a book just filled with *fouls* recipes, there are that many out there...

Cook the beans with the baking soda in a pan of water for around 2 hours until really soft, then drain and mash them with the sesame oil, salt to taste, and spices. Stir in the crumbled cheese.

Fry the eggs and serve the *Shahan Fouls* with the eggs on top and the chopped vegetables in separate bowls so your fellow breakfasters can help themselves. Oh, and you'll need some warm moppy bread to go alongside.

Shalgam-bi-Dibs
TURNIPS WITH DATE SYRUP

GREAT WINTER
SNACK FOR 1

1 tbsp butter
1 medium turnip, peeled and
    cut into thin slices, around
    ⅟₁₆ in/2mm thick
6–8 pitted dates
2 tsp date syrup (if unavailable,
    1 tsp blackstrap molasses
    will do the job)
salt and freshly ground
    black pepper

Dates fried in butter are as close as it gets to dessert nirvana. Except this is a savory dish. Fried dates appear as an unusual accompaniment to all manner of Middle Eastern foods, from chumming up with scrambled egg as a nutritious breakfast to garnishing some of Iran's finest rice dishes.

In this Iraqi recipe, they raise the humble turnip into something pretty awesome. It also works well with parsnips and summer or winter squash, and is a good way of using up the sad unloved vegetables at the bottom of your fridge.

Heat the butter in a small frying pan and sauté the turnip slices for a few minutes on each side. When they start to color, add the dates, stirring well. Cook for a few more minutes, or until the turnips are quite soft, then stir in the date syrup. Bring to a boil, season to taste, and serve.

Timtimo

EAST AFRICAN SPICED RED LENTILS

You know about fridge food, right? It's food that you make to keep in the fridge. Designated, cook-ahead snack fare, if you like. When you are a busy shopkeeper with a snack-monster husband, you need to think about these things.

This is basically an Ethiopian recipe, and would normally be served with *Injera* (see p.142), but most East African countries prepare something similar. Although it is spicy, it is wondrously comforting.

FRIDGE FOOD—
ENOUGH FOR 4
2 medium onions, chopped
sesame oil (untoasted) or peanut oil, for frying
2–3 garlic cloves, chopped
1¼ cups/9oz/250g red lentils, rinsed

2 tbsp *berbere* spice mix (recipe handily
    provided below)
6–7 fresh tomatoes, peeled and chopped (or
    use 1 can/14oz/400g chopped tomatoes)
1¾ cups/400ml water
salt and freshly ground black pepper

Fry the onions in a little oil; once they have softened, add the garlic, stirring well. Throw the lentils into the pan along with the *berbere*. Mix well, then add the tomatoes and water. Bring to a boil, turn down the heat, and simmer for around 30 minutes, adding more water if necessary: the lentils should be soft but not quite dissolved. Season to taste and eat with warm bread and thick yogurt. Like the best fridge food, this actually tastes better the next day, although you may need to add a little more water to it when you reheat it.

*BONUS RECIPE: *BERBERE*

Spice-wise, every region has its "house" mix: in Morocco, there's *ras el hanout*; in Iraq there is *baharat*; next door in Iran there are various generic *adviehs*; go further East and you have garam masala… In Ethiopia and Eritrea, *berbere* is the favored seasoning: a hot and pungent spice mix or paste to use on, well, just about anything.

To make just enough to play with, toast 1 tbsp fenugreek seeds with 2 cloves, ½ tsp cumin seeds, and 1 tsp coriander seeds. Grind in a mortar and pestle or coffee grinder and add 2 tbsp cayenne pepper, 2 tbsp paprika, 1 level tbsp salt, ½ tsp ground black pepper, ½ tsp ground cardamom, ½ tsp ground nutmeg, 1 tsp ground turmeric, and ½ tsp ground allspice. If you want to cheat, it would probably help you to know that the most important ingredients are the fenugreek and the red peppers: like any spice mix, every village/household makes it differently, and so if you are lacking one or two components, don't panic. Store in an airtight jar until needed.

To make *berbere* paste, mix all of the above ingredients with some olive oil, crushed garlic, and crushed ginger. This can be kept in the fridge for a week or so.

Salads and Cold Mezze

This chapter is perhaps at the very heart of what this book is about. Simple, cold fare, nicely presented to serve as a snack or creatively garnished as *mezze*, and nourishing salads to make in advance and enjoy whenever you're in need of a bite.

While I was working in Spain, we regularly took a trip out to a stunning, largely uninhabited mountain range known as the Sierra Bernia. The very sides of the mountains purred with the sound of wind in the pines, and the wafted smell of wild herbs had a somnolent effect on even the most stressed city visitor. Right at the top there was an old shack, which just occasionally, when the breeze was blowing in the right direction, metamorphosed into a snack bar of sorts. It seemed mostly to be manned by a grandchild/grandfather combo: the former would do the work, and the latter would serenade unsuspecting tourists with appallingly flat flamenco music on an out-of-tune guitar. The place was so utterly charming that one never stopped to query the hygiene of the place (goats had free range of the kitchen), or indeed the menu. Even my mother, who, in my teenage years, I recall being unduly obsessed with rabies and dysentery, dug in with relish. You ate what you were given, and paid what you were told to pay.

On one occasion, we were served *tapas* of crumbly Manchego cheese drizzled with olive oil and some still-warm bread. The old man stopped us just as we were about to dig in, shuffled over to a nearby oregano plant, and returned to crumble fresh herbs over the simple repast. This moment has remained seminal to my understanding of *tapas*, and thus *mezze*: food does not need to be complicated to taste and feel good, and several of the recipes that follow are really little more than serving suggestions. Others require more effort, but will reward you with the knowledge that you have a fridgeful of munchables, or at the very least some pretty impressive *mezze* dishes to tarry over while enjoying the company of friends.

Borani-ye-Bademjun

MAKES A SMALL
BOWLFUL
2 medium eggplants
2 medium onions, peeled
3–4 garlic cloves, peeled
oil, for frying
1 tsp garam masala
1¾ cups/14oz/400g thick,
    plain yogurt
salt and ground black pepper

Tip

This makes a good sandwich
filling and a great *mezze* item. It is
far too good a dish to be the
preserve of pampered royals:
those naturally inclined to
snacking would be well advised
to keep a yogurt dish in their
fridge at all times.

Borani refers to a range of yogurt "dips" named after a very spoiled queen (and apparently inveterate snacker) called Pourandokht. Unlike *çacik/tsatsiki* (yogurt with cucumber and mint) and *must-o-moussir* (yogurt with spring garlic), *borani* dishes are made with cooked vegetables. If you think this rings a bell, the (quite different) Afghan version of this is featured in *The New Middle Eastern Vegetarian: Recipes from Veggiestan.*

Preheat the oven to 375°F/190°C.
Prick the eggplants and bake for around 15 minutes, or until soft. Cool a little.
Reserving half an onion, chop the rest along with the garlic and fry them in a little oil until the onion softens. At this stage, add the garam masala. Cook a little longer before setting these too aside to cool.
Now peel some (but not all) of the skin away from the eggplants (it's good to leave a little on as it gives dishes a chunky homemade feel to them—I am always a little suspicious of perfectly homogenized food). Scoop the eggplant together with the cooled onion/garlic mix into a blender and give it all a very quick whizz (or chop through thoroughly with a knife) before stirring the mixture into the yogurt. Season to taste.
Chop and fry the other half of the onion until it becomes quite crispy and brown, then leave to cool. When it is cool, use it to garnish the *borani*.

Mish

PALESTINIAN CHILI YOGURT SALAD

MAKES A DECENT
BOWLFUL
NOTE: PREPARE 1 DAY
IN ADVANCE
2 tsp fenugreek seeds
2 tsp chili flakes
2½ tbsp olive oil
½ tsp salt
1 unwaxed lemon, washed
generous 2 cups/18oz/500g plain
    yogurt
generous 1 cup/9oz/250g *labneh*
    or cream cheese

This is a rustic Palestinian dish. Not that I know many rustic Palestinians. I made some spicy *tsatsiki* (which I smugly thought was my own invention) in the shop one day, and one of my customers told me about *mish*, which has been eaten in the Middle East for centuries. There is something fun about chili-stoked yogurt dishes: the idea that the yogurt cools as the chili burns as the yogurt cools…

Soak the fenugreek seeds for 36–48 hours, changing the water after the first day. Roughly crush the chili flakes and add them to the oil along with the salt, then set aside for 24 hours so the flavors can mingle.
When you are ready to make the *mish*, drain the fenugreek seeds, then finely dice the lemon, skin and all (yes, really). Beat the yogurt together with the *labneh*, then add the fenugreek seeds, chili oil, and chopped lemon, mixing well. Cover and chill in the fridge overnight. Enjoy with warm bread as a *mezze* dip or as an accompaniment to other dishes.

It's *houmous*, Jim, but not as we know it... Well here's the thing. You cannot possibly write a book about Middle Eastern *mezze* and snacking without including *houmous*. It is as commonly to be found on Snackistani restaurant tables as the salt mill, and holds all number of dishes together. Furthermore, it is a well-known fact that most of the vegetarian population of the universe actually live on the stuff, breakfast, lunch, and dinner. Here is my stock recipe for it with a few variations on the theme. *Houmous*, for all you closet etymologists and pedantic Arabists out there, is actually the Arabic word for chickpeas.

BASIC *HOUMOUS BI TAHINA*

MAKES JUST ENOUGH
FOR TODAY—SHOULD
SERVE 4–6 PEOPLE

scant 1¼ cups/7oz/200g dried
    chickpeas, soaked overnight
4 tbsp *tahina*
2 tbsp really good extra-virgin
    olive oil
juice of 2–3 lemons
about 2–4 garlic cloves
salt and freshly ground
    black pepper

TO SERVE:
olive oil, for frying
paprika

The most important thing about *houmous* is that you eat it as fresh as possible. I would also advise against cheating by using canned or jarred chickpeas—they never have the same flavor. I actually like *houmous* while it is still slightly warm.

Reserve a handful of soaked chickpeas, put the rest in a pan, cover them with water, and bring to a boil. Turn down the heat, allow to bubble for around 10 minutes, then skim off any foam or detritus that has risen to the top. Cook for a further hour, or until they are soft and can easily be squidged between your finger and thumb. (Chickpeas vary, and you may find that you have to cook yours for nearly 2 hours: a pinch of baking soda will accelerate things.) Do not drain, but remove the lid and leave them somewhere for 30 minutes or so to cool a little.

You can do the next part by hand, but it is much easier with a blender. Ladle about half of the chickpeas into a blender, including a good amount of the chickpea cooking water. Add half of the *tahina*, olive oil, lemon juice, and garlic and blend until smoothish, adding more of the cooking water if the mixture is too solid. Repeat with the rest of the ingredients, then mix the 2 batches together well and season to taste.

Heat a little olive oil in a pan and fry the reserved chickpeas, stirring constantly, until they are golden and crisp to bite. Drain them on a piece of paper towel then roll them in a little salt.

Serve the *houmous* on a plate/s; if you bash the bottom of the plate against the palm of your hand the dip will spread evenly across the surface. Sprinkle the fried chickpeas across the *houmous*, and follow it up with a pinch of paprika.

Serve as a dip or a sauce or a sandwich filling.

FANCY *HOUMOUS BI TAHINI*

FANCY *HOUMOUS BI TAHINI* #1
WITH POMEGRANATE AND RED PEPPERS THROWN IN

This is a spicy and piquant version. Make the *houmous* as opposite, but using a scant 1 cup/5½oz/150g chickpeas and just 2 tbsp *tahina* plus 1 tbsp lemon juice. Preheat the oven to 375°F/190°C and roast 2 red bell peppers for around 30 minutes, or until they are quite charred. Place them in a plastic bag for 10 minutes and you will find the skin flakes off easily. Remove the seeds and blend them into the *houmous* along with 2 tbsp pomegranate molasses, ¼ Habanero or Scotch bonnet chili (or other hot pepper), and 1 level tsp ground cumin. Garnish with fresh (or dried) pomegranate seeds, if available.

FANCY *HOUMOUS BI TAHINI* #2
WITH TARRAGON AND OLIVES THROWN IN

This is an intriguing mix of umami-ness. Make your *houmous* exactly as opposite, but using just a scant 1 cup/5½oz/150g chickpeas, and adding 1 tsp dried tarragon together with a scant 1¼ cup/7oz/200g pitted green olives. Season the dip at the end, as olives are invariably salty. Be radical and garnish the dish with … an olive.

MUSHY PEA *HOUMOUS*

Fish and chips and mushy peas; it doesn't get much more British than that, unless you do it the Snackistani way.

Make pita chips by heating pita bread, splitting it, cutting it into triangles, and frying these in oil spiced with coriander, cumin, garlic, and chili powder (drain on paper towel). Make fishy goujons by coating fish striplets firstly in seasoned flour, then egg, and finally breadcrumbs mixed with *za'atar*. Fry until crispy golden (then either keep warm or reheat when required). And then the *pièce de résistance*—mushy pea *houmous* as a dip to go in the middle.

If using marrowfat peas, drain most but not all of the liquid away. Put all the ingredients except the oil and salt in a blender (or a big bowl if you are going to blend it all manually) and mix for 2 minutes: you are aiming for a dip with texture rather than a homogenized green paste. With the machine still running, trickle in the olive oil and season to taste. Chill for 30 minutes, or so (anything with *tahina* in it will thicken considerably in the fridge). Sprinkle with sumac before serving.

Arrange your cooled pita "chips" and hot goujons (plus a few lemon wedges) on a platter with a bowl of pea *houmous* in the middle. Lots of fun.

COMFORT SUPPER FOR 4 (A BIG BOWLFUL WITH ENOUGH LEFT OVER FOR A PACKED LUNCH THE NEXT DAY)

2 small cans (around 12oz/360g drained weight) mushy or marrowfat peas

1½ tbsp *tahina*

1½ tbsp lime juice

½ tsp ground cumin

½ tsp dried mint

½ tsp chili flakes (optional)

2 garlic cloves, peeled

1–2 tbsp olive oil

salt, to taste

sumac, to garnish

Ajvar ve Pinjur
A PAIR OF DIPPY THINGS

Ajvar and *pinjur* sound like Disney penguin names, but they are actually both Eastern European/Turkish relishes, created to preserve the pick of the season so that it can be enjoyed throughout the year. Their precise origin is a little obscure: the etymology denotes Turkish origins, but they are most popular in Macedonia and Serbia. They often get muddled up, and with good reason: *ajvar* is basically a red pepper paste to which some people add eggplants, while *pinjur* is an eggplant dip to which some people add red pepper. Confusing, no?

They are both wonderfully snackable: keep jars of them in your fridge, and you can use them on everything from crackers to pizzas to stir-fries. Another plus point is that they both have a natural affinity with cheese. *Ajvar* and *pinjur* can also be served just as they are, with dippy bread, as part of a *mezze* spread.

Each recipe makes enough for a big bowlful—although in Snackistan households will make HUGE batches of this stuff and "lay it down" for a rainy day.

AJVAR: RED PEPPER SPREAD

8 red bell peppers
2 tbsp best extra-virgin olive oil
4 garlic cloves, chopped
2–3 fresh green chilies,
    chopped (optional)
3 tbsp red wine vinegar
salt, to taste

Grill or oven-bake (at 400°F/200°C) the peppers until their skin is quite charred. Allow them to cool a little then put them in a plastic bag for about 10 minutes. This will cause them to sweat, which makes them easy to peel: you should now be able to flake away the skin with your fingers. Remove the seeds, then blend or chop the peppers—aim for chunky rather than puréed.

Gently heat the oil in a frying pan (extra-virgin olive oil has a low smoke point) and quickly fry the garlic and chilies before tipping the bell peppers in, followed by the vinegar. Stir well, season to taste, and simmer for around 30 minutes. Allow to cool before spooning into a sterilized jar (see p.10). *Ajvar* should keep in the fridge for about two weeks. Favorite usage: dolloped on to warm French bread with some lightly melted goats' cheese.

PINJUR: EGGPLANT DIP

2 large eggplants
2 large tomatoes
2 garlic cloves, minced
½ cup/1¾ oz/50g shelled
    walnuts, roughly chopped
2 tbsp extra-virgin olive oil
juice of ½ lemon
salt, to taste
big handful fresh cilantro,
    chopped

Preheat the oven to 375°F/190°C. Prick the eggplants with a fork in several places and bake them on a baking tray for around 15 minutes. Next, place the tomatoes on the same baking tray and cook with the eggplants for another 20 minutes (until the eggplants are pretty soft) before taking them from the oven.

When they are cool enough to handle, skin the tomatoes. Traditionally the eggplants would also be skinned, but I quite like the artisan (aka lazy) approach and leave the skins on. Blend (briefly) or coarsely chop the vegetables together with the garlic and nuts then whisk in the olive oil and lemon juice. Season to taste, and finally stir in the chopped cilantro. Like *ajvar*, this will keep for a week or two in the fridge. Favorite usage: spread in a pita pocket with fried halloumi.

BEET SALAD WITH CARDAMOM YOGURT DRESSING

Lady Beet has but to lie down on a plate to look effortlessly alluring—if she was a real woman I'd hate her. Jesting aside, you really don't need to do much to this thrifty little root to turn it into a fine snack or *mezze* dish, and this salad is nothing if not simple.

MEZZE PLATTER
OR APPETIZER FOR 6

3 medium beets

scant ½ cup /100ml plain, runny yogurt
  (runny usually = cheap)

2 tbsp olive oil

1 tbsp *sekanjebin** (optional—you could just
  use 1 fat tsp honey instead)

1 tbsp apple cider vinegar

1 level tsp ground cardamom

¾ in/2cm piece fresh ginger, peeled
  and minced

salt and freshly ground black pepper

handful of fresh mint, shredded

Preheat the oven to 400°F/200°C.

Top and tail the beets, retaining any of the prettier parts of foliage still attached, then wrap them in foil and bake for around 1½ hours, or until they are tender when prodded. Unwrap and allow to cool a little.

When the beets are cool enough to handle, slice into ⅛ in/3mm (ish) thick rounds and arrange on a pretty platter. You can enjoy this salad at any temperature you like: still-warm works for us.

Whisk the yogurt together with the oil, *sekanjebin*, vinegar, spices, and seasoning before drizzling it artistically over the beets. Strew the shredded mint over it along with any retained beet tops. Try not to drool: it is very unbecoming.

*BONUS RECIPE: *SEKANJEBIN*
(THAT'S IRANIAN MINT AND VINEGAR SYRUP TO YOU)

1½ cups/350ml water

1¾ cups/350g sugar

4 tbsp white vinegar

a dozen sprigs of fresh mint, shredded

Handy hint

If, like me, you enjoy beets with a little too much gusto, be advised that white vinegar and cold water and baking soda go a long way towards removing beet stains.

This stuff is so useful—I sneak it into all kinds of recipes. You can buy it in Middle Eastern stores, but it takes just 10 minutes to make your own…

Place the water in a pan, add the sugar, and bring to a boil. Bubble for 10 minutes, remove from the heat, and add the vinegar. When it is a bit cooler, add the mint, bottle, and chill.

MOROCCAN RAW TURNIP SALAD

CRUNCHY *MEZZE*
FOR 4 (OR A SUPER-
HEALTHY WINTER
LUNCH FOR
1 VIRTUOUS SOUL)

5 tbsp good olive oil

juice and grated zest of 1 lime

½ tsp ground cumin

1 tsp ground coriander

½ tsp ground cinnamon

1 tsp ground paprika

1 tsp dried dill

salt

4 pert-looking baby turnips,
    peeled and very thinly sliced

½ cup/1¾ oz/50g slivered
    almonds

1 small pomegranate (really juicy,
    preferably Iranian or Turkish)

big bunch of watercress

1 medium red onion, cut
    into slices

½ tsp ground black pepper

"Do not crawl into a turnip furrow and open your mouth: the turnip cannot accompany you in wit or on journeys..." (Rumi)

... it is, however, really healthy fare, even when cooked. The turnip is a much overlooked little guy, but it is cheap, full of nutrients, and great for chesty colds. We should be eating it more often.

Raw stuff. It's real fashionable right now—and by all accounts much better for us. But if I am honest, I still experience a little frisson of danger every time I eat something raw that I have spent my life eating cooked. This turnip salad recipe is a good example.

It is based on something I had in Morocco (um, hence the name of the dish), but improvised with an added Persian twist. It is pleasingly red, white, and green, and so would make for good yuletide fare.

Whisk 3 tablespoons of the olive oil together with the lime juice, spices, dill, and a pinch of salt. Place the turnips in a plastic bowl and cover them with the spiced oil. Mix well, cover, and chill for 1–2 hours.

Put the almonds on a baking tray and toast in the oven (at 375°F/190°C) for around 10 minutes, or until lightly golden in color.

Just before you are ready to eat, pummel the pomegranate all over with your thumbs, taking care not to break the skin: it should end up quite soft and squidgy under the skin. Make a small incision in the skin and invert the hole over a glass: if you squeeze very gently, the juice released by your pummeling should flow into the glass. Now that the tension is released, you should be able to break the fruit open and scoop all the intact, remaining seeds into a bowl (take care not to include any pith).

Pile some watercress into your salad bowl, then scatter some of the marinated turnips (and the marinade) over it. Top with some of the onion and pomegranate seeds, and repeat until all the ingredients have been layered up. Finally, scatter the almonds over the top.

Beat the remaining olive oil together with the extracted pomegranate juice, black pepper, and salt to taste, and then drizzle it over the salad.

MARINATED ASPARAGUS

MEZZE OR REFINED
SNACKING FOR 4–6

1–2 bunches of asparagus,
    woody white ends
    chopped off
scant ½ cup/100ml extra-virgin
    olive oil
juice and grated zest of 2 lemons
2 garlic cloves, minced
sea salt and freshly ground
    black pepper
2 tsp *za'atar* (see p.16), optional

Some vegetables are so extraordinarily special that they do not brook much fancy meddling. One such is asparagus.

Although the word is derived from the Persian word *asparagh* (sprout), it is not commonly enjoyed in the eastern reaches of Snackistan. But it has been popular around the Mediterranean for centuries and the Romans couldn't get enough of it.

Blanch the asparagus in boiling water for around 3 minutes before draining and plunging into icy cold water.

Whisk the oil, lemon, garlic, seasoning, and *za'atar* together. Place the drained asparagus in a tub, bathe it in the marinade, cover, and chill for 2–3 hours. Share, if you must.

AVOCADO AND YOGURT DIP WITH SUMAC

MAKES ENOUGH FOR
A BIG BOWLFUL

2 large ripe avocados
    (or 3–4 small ones)
generous 1 cup/9oz/250g thick,
    plain live/probiotic yogurt
2 tomatoes (softish ones will do),
    quartered
2 garlic cloves, peeled
big handful of fresh cilantro
½ tsp ground cumin
½ tsp ground coriander
1 generous tsp ground sumac,
    plus extra to garnish
½ tsp chili powder (or more if
    you're a bit of a pepper-head)
grated zest and juice of 1 lime
glug of olive oil
salt, to taste

Ah now. Avocado. Known across the region as, um, avocado. It is certainly not indigenous to Snackistan, but it has nevertheless become ubiquitous across the region over the last 100 years or so. And it is via Snackistan—Israel, to be precise—that they came to the UK. Bizarrely, I can remember my mother going to a product launch party for housewives in the 1970s: it was organized by Carmel with a view to introducing this wondrous new "fruit." I guess it made a change from Tupperware and coffee mornings. Not that she'll admit to having attended such things.

Not only is avocado tasty, slightly fancy, and a very pretty shade of green, it is good for you. It is very oily, but the oil is all good stuff, and the fruit is now widely believed to reduce cholesterol. Inclusion of more avocado in your diet (reputedly) has long-term benefits for both skin and hair.

Sumac has slightly antibacterial properties, and if you use a good probiotic yogurt, that makes this a really healthy snack.

Peel the avocados and remove the stones. Plop them in a blender along with all the other ingredients and whizz for a few seconds. I like this dip all artisanal and chunky, but if you want pureé, then blend it a bit more.

Garnish with some extra sprinkled sumac and serve with hot pita bread and crudités. Or if you are a peasant like myself, you could just eat it with a spoon straight from the bowl.

ON ONE-VEGGIE SALADS

"Recipes" like the asparagus recipe can be applied to practically any vegetable (and quite a lot of fruit, cold meat, fish, and cheese as well). There are very few ingredients that are not improved by the addition of olive oil, lemon juice, salt, and pepper. Some of them benefit from marinating therein, other ingredients just need a sauce or dressing to perk them up and turn them from something mundane into an eminently snackable dish. Some need blanching to make them easy to eat, others are just fine and dandy raw. Add a few herbs, or spices, or honey, or mustard, or any number of bits and pieces from your pantry, and you have a dish fit for hungry kings.

Here's a short list of vegetables that respond well to being marinated:
  Artichokes: blanch first, work well with thyme and garlic
  Cauliflower/broccoli: use raw, both respond well to spices and *tahina*
  Cucumbers: use raw, and rather obviously with oil, vinegar, and dill
  Eggplants: cook first, love a sweet and sour treatment

Fava (broad) beans: blanch and shuck, come out a treat with lemon, garlic, dill, and saffron
Mushrooms: use raw, great pals with tarragon
Onions: use hot vinegar with juniper/thyme
Swiss chard: raw is fine, prefers vinegar to lemon juice
Tomatoes: raw, love all herbs, especially basil and mint
Zucchini: use raw, need lots of garlic and lemon

Root vegetables are often better cooked and dressed (rather than marinated), but a lot of traditional salads using these are very complicated and heavy (think sour cream and mayonnaise). Try whisking olive oil, lemon juice, oregano or dill, mustard or horseradish, salt, and pepper together. Simple.

Most beans and legumes also need cooking: in Turkey, there is a whole range of very simple dishes which are collectively known as *zeytinyagli*, or "olive oily dishes." Beans, leeks, eggplants, and all sorts of veggies are cooked slowly with an unfeasible amount of olive oil, then served warm or cold as *mezze*—naughty, but nice.

Maash Pulao

SPICED BROWN RICE AND MUNG BEAN SALAD

Maash Pulao is a popular Afghan dish, although it is also enjoyed across Transoxiana (northeastern Iran and Central Asia). But the dish is generally served hot, with or without meaty chunks added. Here it is turned into something else entirely.

Rice salad at buffet parties, frankly, used to give me the willies. Boiled Uncle Ben's with some defrosted frozen vegetables shoved in. You should find this *mezze*/lunchbox-filler altogether more interesting…

SIDE DISH OR *MEZZE* PLATTER FOR 6

1¼ cups/9oz/250g brown basmati rice
scant ½ cup/2¾oz/75g dried apricots
½ cup/3½oz/100g mung beans
butter (or ghee)
salt
2 good tsp garam masala
1 bunch of scallions, chopped
3oz/80g radishes, sliced
½ cup/3oz/80g pistachio halves
　(or use pumpkin seeds)
2 tbsp mango pickle (yes, you can substitute
　another pickle—mango is just better)
3 tbsp olive oil
1 tbsp apple vinegar
salt and freshly ground black pepper
½ bunch of fresh cilantro, chopped

Soak the rice for around 30 minutes: this is not essential, but in the case of brown rice it does make for a softer end product/less cooking time. At the same time, set the apricots to soak in a separate bowl of water.

Put the mung beans in a pan of cold water and bring to a boil; they take about 25 minutes to cook.

While the beans are cooking, boil or steam the rice with butter and salt according to your preferred method.* Drain if necessary, stir the garam masala through it, mixing thoroughly, and set it aside to cool.

Meanwhile, back in the bean pan: you should cook the mung beans until they are edible without being mushy, then run some cold water over them to arrest the cooking process. Drain and reserve.

Drain and chop the apricots and mix them with the cooled rice, beans, onions, radishes, and nuts in a bowl. Whisk the pickle, oil, and vinegar together with a little salt and pepper and pour it over the *Maash Pulao*, stirring well. Finally, toss the cilantro through the salad: this is done at the last moment to preserve the pretty green-ness of the herbs. Check the seasoning and serve. This is one of my favorite shop lunches: full of good things, easily digestible, and no garlic to scare the customers away.

✳ Handy tip

Here's my preferred all-purpose method for cooking rice, if it helps: Use 1 measure of rice to 1 measure of water (a standard rice-cooker measuring cup holds around ¾ cup/5½oz/150g of rice and ¾ cup/200ml of water) plus 2 teaspoons butter (or ghee) and salt to taste. Rinse the rice well. Put the water, butter, and salt in a pan and bring it to a boil. Add the rice, bubble away for a few minutes, then turn down the heat really low, wrap the lid of the pan in a clean cloth, and simmer for another 20 minutes. The rice should be perfectly cooked and the grains perfectly separated. Let it sit, covered, for 5–10 minutes more before fluffing with a fork and serving.

PEARL COUSCOUS AND BLACK CUMIN SALAD

SERVES 6

olive oil, for frying
    (not extra-virgin)
1 good tsp black cumin seeds
½ tsp chili flakes
about ⅝ in/1.5cm piece fresh
    ginger, peeled and minced
7oz/200g pearl couscous
a generous 2 cups/500ml
    good vegetable stock
    (or good water)
3 tbsp extra-virgin olive oil
2 tsp *pekmez* (grape syrup)
1 tbsp balsamic vinegar
salt
1 bunch of scallions, chopped
½ bunch of fresh cilantro,
    chopped
around 24 dates, pitted and
    roughly chopped
4oz/120g *labneh* balls,
    roughly crumbled

The black cumin myth

This is regular cumin's very elite cousin. It is also known as black caraway. Black cumin is not the same as *Nigella sativa*, and neither of these are related to the *Allium* family, which makes the nickname "black onion seeds" (with which both get labeled) confusing at best. Black cumin is slightly sweet, packed full of nutrients, and aids the digestion. It is used mostly in Iranian and Central Asian cuisine, and is deployed to great effect in *zireh pulao*, a fragrant rice dish.

Well, this has got our store and supper club customers talking, and so we thought we'd share the recipe with you. It is spicy, filling, and healthy, and so it's perfect for winter snacking. It also makes a great *mezze* dish.

Pearl or giant couscous is also known as Israeli couscous, but is confusingly not as giant as *moghrabbieh*, its Levantine cousin. It is easier to work with than *moghrabbieh*, as it is not as starchy, but it gets just as many "oohs" and "aahs" when you dish it up as it looks, well, like toy food. Not entirely real.

You can of course make this recipe with any number of grains in place of the couscous. And if you can't get crubly *labneh* balls, just use feta in its place. Black cumin seeds have a fairly unique flavor, but if you can't find them, just substitute green cumin and caraway seeds. Oh and finally, if you can't find *pekmez* (which is available at all good Greek and Turkish stores), just replace it with pomegranate paste, or (if you're desperate) steak sauce mixed with extra balsamic vinegar. Why so many alternative ingredient ideas? Because food should never be that stressy, and you should never be slave to a recipe: if you can't get the right stuff, cheat.

So all you do is… heat the oil in a saucepan and toss in the spices and ginger, stirring constantly. Have the extractor fan on or the window open, as sizzling hot pepper can make you choke. After 30 seconds, add the couscous, mixing well. Turn it over in the oil until it starts to brown, then trickle in a little of the stock (just as you would with a risotto). Once the liquid has been absorbed, add a little bit more; repeat until the couscous has swollen and softened. This process should take no more than 20 minutes. Wrap the lid of the pan in a clean cloth, turn the heat off, and let the contents "sweat" for a further 10 minutes before setting the pan aside somewhere to cool.

Once it has cooled to room temperature or thereabouts, whisk the extra-virgin olive oil, *pekmez*, balsamic vinegar, and salt together and pour it over the couscous, stirring well, then add the rest of the ingredients. (By dressing it first then adding the herbs and cheese, the contrasting colors will be preserved for a little longer.)

Serve with warm bread for dinner, or as part of a *mezze*. Or spoon it into your finest Tupperware for lunch tomorrow.

WARM EGGPLANT SALAD WITH CHILIED *TAHINI*

Eggplants and *tahini*: a match made in *jannah* (Arabic heaven). Eggplant is to all intents and purposes edible blotting paper: it absorbs any flavors you care to throw at it.

SNACK DINNER FOR 2:
ALSO GOOD FOR LADIES
WHO *MEZZE*-LUNCH

2 medium eggplants,
    cut into ¾–1¼ in/2–3cm cubes
2 small red onions,
    cut into ¾–1¼ in/2–3cm cubes
olive oil
1–1½ tsp lemon salt (citric acid)
6 garlic cloves (less if you have an important
    meeting in the morning), peeled and
    "bruised" (bash swiftly with the flat part
    of a chopping knife)

3 tbsp *tahina*
1 tbsp lemon juice
around ⅔ cup/150ml cold water
½ tsp chili flakes
salt, to taste
1–2 tbsp sesame seeds (2 if you are like me
    and can never get enough of the things)
big handful of fresh parsley and mint, chopped

Preheat the oven to 350°F/180°C.

Arrange the eggplants and onions on a baking tray. Drizzle with olive oil, sprinkle with the lemon salt, and bake uncovered for around 20 minutes; then add the garlic and cook for a further 20 minutes, or until the vegetables are tender and turning brown.

Meanwhile, whisk the *tahina* together with the lemon juice and beat in enough cold water to make a drizzle-able paste. Add the chili flakes and salt as required, and chill until needed. Time too to toast the sesame seeds: dry-fry them for a few minutes until they start to brown then set aside.

When the eggplant is cooked, arrange it on a plate. Trickle the *tahini* over it, then sprinkle with sesame seeds and chopped herbs. Serve with warm bread to mop it up.

Salata Duco

SAUDI CILANTRO SALSA

This is sooo simple. Easy-peasy lemon-or-lime-squeezy. It is pretty wholesome eaten on its own, but it makes a great cooling accompaniment to other rich *mezze* plates, not to mention kebabs. It is the Arabian answer to *fattoush*, the classic Lebanese dish made with stale bread, or *salad-e-Shirazi*, which is the quintessential Persian salad, made like *ducos*, but with onion and cucumber as well.

Sear the tomatoes over a lit gas burner, or plunge them into boiling water: either method will have the desired result of allowing you to peel them (probably best let them cool a little first). Chop the tomato flesh finely into a bowl, taking care to retain all the juice.

Roughly chop the cilantro, chilies, and garlic if using, then pound them together with the salt in a mortar and pestle. If you don't own a mortar and pestle (I don't, but don't tell any of my foodie friends), then put the herb/chili/garlic/salt mixture on a chopping board, cover it with a clean cloth, and grind it using a chunky utensil handle. Mix the resultant green gloop into the tomatoes and dress with the lime or lemon juice. Add more salt as required. Best consumed within a few hours.

MAKES A LITTLE BOWLFUL
4 large tomatoes (soft ones will do nicely)
small bunch of fresh cilantro, trimmed
2–3 green chilies
2 garlic cloves, peeled (optional)
½ tsp salt (celery salt works best here, but is not authentic)
juice of 2 limes (or lemons)

CABBAGE WITH SUMAC

To make a healthy change from coleslaw: in addition to its obvious casting as part of a *mezze* spread, this performs well at barbecues. This is based on a Georgian recipe.

Blanch the cabbage in boiling water for just 1 minute before draining then plunging it into cold water to arrest the cooking process. Drain it once again and put it in a bowl.

Next, whisk the olive oil together with the garlic, sumac, and seasoning and pour it over the cabbage, stirring well. Cover the bowl and leave it in the fridge for 2 hours.

Just before you're ready to serve, dry toast the hemp (or sesame) and caraway seeds in a small pan for a minute or so. Arrange the cabbage (marinade 'n' all) on a pretty plate and sprinkle with the still-warm seeds.

MEZZE FOR 4
around 1lb 5oz/600g (roughly half a head) cabbage, shredded (red, green, or white … or all three if you're feeling extravagant)
scant ¼ cup/50ml extra-virgin olive oil
2 garlic cloves, minced
1½ tsp sumac
sea salt and freshly ground black pepper (according to preference)
1 tbsp hemp seeds (or use sesame)
1 level tsp caraway seeds

Mostly Carbs

"Saturn was sighted before the creation of the heavens; bread was sighted before grain." (Rumi)

What Snackistanis eat when they are showing off is rice, which is regarded as a sophisticated carbohydrate; what they eat when they are chilling, or snacking, or out in the streets is bread-based. Because they invented bread, and they've been eating it in one form or another for millennia.

Generalization though this may be, it is fair to say that most Middle Eastern towns and villages have a bakery on every other corner. Fresh flatbread is eaten throughout the day with breakfast, lunch, and dinner; it is wrapped, dipped, dunked, crumbled, stuffed, rolled and finally recycled into other dishes. It is the beginning and end of most Middle Eastern meals and snacks. And so most of this chapter is dedicated to bread and stuff that resembles bread.

Mana'eesh
LEBANESE STREET PIZZA BREAD

MAKES 15

For the basic dough:

1 envelope (¼ oz/7g) active dry
yeast (or ½ oz/14g fresh)

pinch of sugar

generous 1 cup/250ml lukewarm
water

3½ cups/1lb 2oz/500g
all-purpose flour

1 tsp salt

1–2 tbsp olive oil

Mana'eesh is a popular Lebanese street snack: part open sandwich, part mini pizza. At its simplest, it is just a particularly flavorsome bread. Get creative and you've got a whole range of canapés, picnic, and party possibilities open to you.

I offer three toppings: the first is the most traditional, *za'atar*. The second is a Syrian version, using the *dukkah* topping. The third, *laham b'ajeen*, involves ground lamb (p.140).

Dissolve the yeast and sugar in the warm water and set aside for 10 minutes.

Sift the flour and salt into a mixing bowl and make a well in the middle. Now add the yeast-water combo, mixing at first with a wooden spoon, then, when the ingredients come together, your hands. Form the dough into a ball and roll it in a little oil to keep it moist. Cover it with a damp cloth and leave somewhere warm for 2 hours to rise.

When risen, knead the mixture with verve, vim, and vigor on a floured work surface, then divide it into 15 balls. Leave the dough to rise for a further 15 minutes, then pull them into small flat rounds with your hands and spread them out on 1 or 2 oiled baking trays.

Preheat the oven to 450°F/230°C.

Bake the bread rounds for 8–10 minutes, or until they are slightly risen and lightly browned. These will keep for several days in a covered plastic tub, and can be eaten hot or cold. This bread/pastry is kinda soft, and so can also be warmed in a microwave.

ZA'ATAR TOPPING

Za'atar is one of the most famous Snackistani spice/condiment blends. Every town and village across the Levant makes it differently, but it is basically a mixture of wild thyme (which is in itself known as *za'atar*) with sumac, sesame, and salt. You can buy it easily enough in good Middle Eastern stores now, but it is also simple to make. Grind 2 parts thyme (in the absence of real wild thyme) with 1 part sumac, a handful of sesame seeds, and salt to taste. To turn it into a distinctive and aromatic bread or pizza topping, mix the spices with olive oil to form a paste, then smear the paste across the raw *mana'eesh* dough just before you cook it. The addition of grated mozzarella or halloumi is an authentic optional extra.

DUKKAH: A REALLY GREAT TOPPING

Dukkah is used both as a condiment in Arabic countries and as a snack in its own right. It is basically a coarse-ground spicy nut/seed mix, but it is very tasty and can be used in all sorts of culinary contexts. The original recipe calls for equal quantities of raw hazelnuts and sesame seeds, together with half that amount of cumin and coriander seeds. You toast all the ingredients together, then crush them coarsely and season to taste with sea salt and coarsely ground black pepper. For this recipe, I vary it slightly by using ⅓ cup/1¾oz/50g each of sunflower, sesame, and pumpkin seeds, and ⅓ cup/1¾oz/50g hazelnuts or almonds. Add 1 tbsp each of cumin, coriander, and fenugreek seeds, then toast, season, and blend.

Laham b'ajeen
PIQUANT LAMB TOPPED PIZZAS

MAKES AROUND 15

1 large onion, chopped

oil, for cooking

3 large tomatoes, chopped

1 tsp ground allspice

½ tsp red pepper powder
   (optional)

2 tbsp pomegranate molasses
   (or lemon juice)

12oz/350g ground lamb (leaner
   cuts are better for this)

½ tsp salt

½ tsp ground black pepper

scant ½ cup/2¼ oz/60g pine nuts

1 quantity *mana'eesh* dough,
   pounded and proofed (p.138)

I am very fond of these little pizza pies. One or two make a great snack, and every shop on London's Edgware Road seems to sell them.

Fry the onion in a splosh of oil. Once it has softened, add the tomatoes and cook through so that most of the tomato juice evaporates. Add the spices and pomegranate molasses (or lemon juice), take off the heat, and cool to room temperature.

Preheat the oven to 450°F/230°C.

Mix the raw ground lamb with the cooled onion mix, seasoning, and pine nuts, pounding well. Form the dough into 15 small circles, as per the recipe on p.138, and distribute the raw lamb mixture between them, spreading it thinly. Bake for around 10 minutes, or until sizzling and brown around the edges. Eat hot or cold: if you are enjoying them fresh out of the oven, try rolling them around a handful of fresh herbs (see p.162). They will keep for 1–2 days in the fridge.

SEEDED BROCCOLI *SFIHA*

MAKES 15

scant ⅓ cup/1¾ oz/50g raisins

2 medium heads of broccoli,
   broken into small florets

2 medium red onions, finely
   sliced

oil, for frying

2 garlic cloves, minced (optional)

2 tbsp balsamic vinegar

1 tsp brown sugar

salt and freshly ground black
   pepper

1 quantity *mana'eesh* dough,
   pounded and proofed (p.138)

grated halloumi or mozzarella
   (optional non-vegan topping)

2–3 tbsp Snackistani *dukkah* mix
   (see p.138)

Sfiha is yet another version of *mana'eesh*, this time from Syria. It uses the same dough, but is formed more like an eccentric tart. The conventional filling is lamb, as per the *Laham b'ajeen* recipe above, but I like this veggie/vegan version.

Soak the raisins while you make the rest of the filling.

Blanch the broccoli in boiling water for around 2 minutes, then drain and refresh it under cold water.

Fry the onions in a little oil until they are soft and nicely browned, then add the garlic and (drained) raisins, stirring well for 2 minutes. Next, add the vinegar and sugar and a little seasoning, and let the mixture bubble gently for about 5 minutes before taking off the heat.

Preheat the oven to 450°F/230°C. Lightly oil a couple of baking trays.

Divide your proofed *mana'eesh* dough into about 15 balls and allow them to rise for another 10 minutes before pulling and pressing them into flat discs. Put a spoonful of broccoli in the middle of each, followed by a covering of the caramelized onion mixture. Sprinkle a little grated cheese on top, if using. Taking one of the discs, pinch the edges of the dough in four places so that it folds up to form a square-ish tart (the rim should be just ¼in/5–6mm high), and slide it onto the baking tray. Repeat with the rest of the *sfiha* and bake them for around 15 minutes, or until the pastry is just starting to turn a pleasant golden color. Remove from the oven, sprinkle liberally with *dukkah*, and serve hot, warm, or cold. These keep for 2–3 days in the fridge.

Injera

ETHIOPIAN PANCAKE BREAD

Injera is a lot more than a bread: it is a whole concept and one that is seminal to the Ethiopian way of eating. And Ethiopia is in East Africa, right next to Saudi Arabia, so it's an honorary part of Snackistan, right? Ethiopian cooking is one of the most exciting cuisines in the world, as it has remained largely uncorrupted by the scourge of colonization.

Injera is a really friendly, fun-loving carbohydrate. You see, it's used as a tablecloth: an edible tablecloth. You just plonk it on top of a little (traditionally round, low-lying) table, and ladle your food on top. No knives or forks or plates: no dishwashing. Just break off a bit of the tablecloth, and use it to scoop up the dish of your choice. Perfect for *mezze* and snacking. In Ethiopia, it is usually served with *wat*, or stew, but we like to dot it with dips, salads, and marinated vegetables.

It is traditionally made from *teff*, a teensy-weensy millet-like grain. *Teff* has been grown in East Africa for thousands of years, and is particularly suited to the nomadic lifestyle as it springs up pretty quickly and doesn't need pampered soil in which to do its thing. It's often tricky to find in the West, but the flavor and the experience is easily replicated using flour and sparkling water.

This version is pleasingly easy to make: no messing around with yeast, which I always find a little nerve-wracking, no need to leave the dough to ferment, and no need even for an oven.

MAKES ENOUGH FOR
A SNACK DINNER FOR 4

¾ cup /3½ oz/100g self-rising flour

scant ⅔ cup/3½ oz/100g whole-wheat flour

1 tsp baking powder

pinch of salt

1¾ cups/400ml sparkling or soda water

juice of 1 lemon

a smidge of vegetable oil

Sift the first four ingredients together, then mix in the sparkling water and the lemon juice, beating to a smooth paste. If it is too thick, just add a little more water.

Using a brush or a piece of paper towel, coat a large non-stick frying pan with oil and put it on the heat. Drizzle the batter mix in, swirling it from the center out to the edge until the bottom of the pan is evenly covered. Allow it to cook through until little holes start to appear on the surface, then remove from the pan with a wooden spatula. The result should be just cooked through on the bottom, but still spongy on top. Keep the cooked *injera* warm by covering with foil until you are ready to serve.

Repeat with the rest of the mixture—you should have enough for about 5–6 breads, which you can then piecemeal together to make a quilted spread.

Injera will keep until the next day if you wrap it in a clean cloth or plastic bag.

Mujadarra
RICE AND LENTILS

This I could probably live on. It is the sort of food that you just have to keep on eating until you are ready to burst.

Mujadarra is actually the Arabic word for smallpox. But you should not let this put you off—it merely refers to the appearance of the rice studded with lentils. It has in all likelihood been eaten for millennia in the Middle East, although the original dish was almost certainly made with bulgar (cracked wheat) rather than rice. An ancient urban myth has it that this is the original "mess of pottage" for which Esau sold his soul in the Bible. Versions of it are made across modern Snackistan: in Iran, *adass pulao* (spiced rice with lentils and fried fruit) is served as an accompaniment, while in Egypt *kushari* (rice, lentils, and pasta) is one of the nation's favorite street foods.

It is simple and cheap to make: perfect thrifty-student, comfort, or snack fare.

COMFORT EATING FOR 4–6

1¼ cups/9oz/250g brown lentils

4 medium onions, peeled

oil, for frying

1 tsp ground coriander

1 tsp ground cumin

1¼ cups/9oz/250g long-grain brown rice

salt and freshly ground black pepper

generous pat of butter (or vegan alternative)

Put the lentils in a pan of unsalted water, bring it to a boil, then turn down the heat, and simmer for about 15 minutes before draining and setting aside.

Finely chop 2 of the onions and fry them in a little oil. Once they have turned translucent, add the spices and rice, stirring well, followed by the par-cooked lentils. Add just enough water to the pan to only just cover the contents, then bring to a boil, turn down the heat, and simmer for around 20 minutes, or until all the water has been absorbed (use a heat diffuser here if you have one—it helps when you are cooking stuff, such as rice and wheat, slowly and by absorption). Now turn off the heat and season the rice mix to taste. Wrap the lid of the pan in a clean dish towel and cover the *mujadarra*: it will continue to cook in its own steam while you set the table, feed the cat, light a candle, whatever…

To serve, slice the remaining 2 onions and fry them in butter until they are pretty well browned. Pile the lentilly rice into a dish, top with the buttery onions and serve with pickles, yogurt, and salad.

Laghman
KYRGYZSTANI NOODLES

Laghman is common to all of the Central Asian countries, but seems most frequently enjoyed by Kyrgyzstanis. It is perhaps a reflection of the country's proximity to China as it has decidedly oriental overtones. The dish appears in lots of different formats, from rather soupy with just a few noodles in it, through to what is basically a plate of pasta with a lamb or vegetable topping. This recipe veers towards the latter. You could just serve vinegar as an extra topping, but it is worth the effort to make *laza*, which is a fiery condiment much enjoyed by the folk of the (let's-face-it-rather-chilly) steppes.

The noodles are fun to make—but you could easily substitute linguini if you were pushed for time. You will need somewhere to "dry" the *laghman* noodles: a very clean clothes drying rack would be ideal, but if not they can be draped over the backs of chairs or a Rube Goldberg arrangement of cans, string, and utensils.

SERVES 6–8

FOR THE NOODLES:
5 cups/1lb 10oz/750g all-purpose flour
1 tbsp salt
3 eggs, beaten
3 tbsp butter, melted
1¼ cups/275ml tepid water
8 cups/2 liters vegetable stock

FOR THE TOPPING:
2 medium onions, sliced
butter and a dash of oil, for frying
4 garlic cloves, minced
2 large bell peppers (ideally 1 green
    and 1 red), julienned
3 large carrots, peeled and julienned

1 tsp ground cumin
1 tsp ground coriander
1 star anise, crumbled
pinch of ground cloves
1 tsp black peppercorns, coarsely ground
½ small cabbage, roughly shredded
1 tbsp tomato paste
6 large tomatoes, roughly cut into chunks
2 tbsp red wine (or grape) vinegar
4 cups/1 liter water

FOR THE *LAZA* SAUCE:
2 tbsp sunflower oil
2 tbsp crushed dried chili peppers
1 tsp salt
6 garlic cloves, minced
2 tbsp wine vinegar

Sift the flour and salt into a bowl, then beat in the eggs, butter, and water with a wooden spoon. The dough should come together to form a ball: if it looks dry, add a little more water. Knead the dough for about 5 minutes, cover with a damp cloth, and leave somewhere warm to rise for about an hour.

Once the dough has had an hour to proof, turn it out on to a floured board and knead it some more before dividing it into 4 (more or less) equal balls. Flour your rolling pin then roll out the first ball into a rough rectangular shape, about $\frac{1}{16}$–$\frac{1}{8}$ in/2–3mm thick.

[method continues on p.147]

Cut the dough into strips lengthways, then take each strip in turn, grasping it at either end, and spin it so that it stretches like elastic. Dust each elongated noodle with extra flour, and as you finish each one, dangle it over your drying rack, or improvised version thereof. Repeat with the rest of the strips, then roll out the other dough balls. Leave the noodles to dry for around an hour.

Meanwhile, make the topping. Fry the onions in a pat of butter with a dash of oil. Once they have turned translucent, add the garlic, peppers, and carrots and cook for around 5 minutes, stirring regularly, before adding the spices and cabbage, followed a few minutes later by the tomato paste and fresh tomato. After a few minutes more, add the vinegar and water, bring to a boil, then turn down the heat and simmer for around 30 minutes.

Prepare the *laza* by heating the sunflower oil until sizzle hot. Put the chili, salt, and garlic in a heatproof bowl, add the vinegar, and pour the sizzling oil over it. Mix and allow to cool; if not using straight away, bottle and keep in the fridge—*laza* will keep for several weeks and can be used to, um, "perk up" any number of dishes.

Time to cook the pasta. Bring the vegetable stock to a boil in a big pan and cook the noodles for around 5 minutes, draining and refreshing them in cold water very briefly (you may need to work in 2–3 batches, in which case use tongs to extract the noodles from the boiling stock). Once cooked, pile the noodles into a bowl and spoon the topping over them—the heat of the topping should be enough to warm the noodles once again. You could also serve the noodles and topping separately, in which case you will have to reheat the noodles by either flashing them in a microwave or frying them in a little oil.

Serve the *laza* on the side, perhaps with a danger warning attached: it is really hot stuff.

GARLIC, EGGPLANT, AND GINGER *PAKORA*

Pakora are fritters. Spicy fritters. Yup—just like the ones you get at Indian restaurants. Except these ones are based on an Afghan recipe. They are popular street food in the main -istans, and are very easy to make at home. You can of course make them with any vegetable.

Cut the eggplants into slices of ½in/1cm thickness, arrange them on a tray, and rub them with a scant amount of salt. Set them aside for around 30 minutes.

Make the batter: sift the flour into a bowl with the spices and seasoning and slowly add the ginger beer, whisking all the while. This too will benefit from 30 minutes' "rest."

Ready to cook? Wipe the eggplant firmly with some paper towel, then chop the garlic with ½ teaspoon salt, and rub the mixture over the eggplant slices. Whisk the batter again, and heat at least 1½in/4cm oil in a frying pan. Dip the eggplant into the batter, allowing any surplus to drain back into the bowl, and fry each of the slices until they are golden brown. Drain on paper towel and serve hot with chutney or yogurt. These are best eaten fresh as they don't reheat very well.

SERVES 8

2 large eggplants

salt

1¾ cups/9oz/250g chickpea (gram) flour

½ tsp ground ginger

½ tsp ground cumin

1 tsp ground coriander

1 tsp mustard seeds

½ tsp ground fenugreek (nice, but optional)

½ tsp ground black pepper

pinch of salt

about ⅔ can ginger beer

4 garlic cloves

sunflower or canola oil, for frying

ON *CARAVANSERAI*:
THE ORIGINAL DRIVE-THROUGHS...

Imagine a place where you could meet new people, trade items, exchange ideas, arrange for food and supplies, unwind after a hard day's work... No, it's not the Internet, but something that could easily be regarded as its forerunner: the *caravanserai*.

It is in fact another fine Persian invention. Yes—my Iranian husband does pay me to say these things, but the very word "caravan" is derived from the Persian word *karban*, which kind of means "to protect trade." *Caravanserai* means "a house of protected trade," and these famous Middle Eastern watering holes were exactly that: ancient motels for traveling salesmen. The oriental name for them is *khan*, while the Arabs call them *funduq*: they do not actually belong to any one period or nation, but were evolved over millennia the length and breadth of the trade routes (most notably the Silk Road). The most prolific builders thereof were the Turkish Seljuks (in the Middle Ages) and the Iranian Safavids (in the sixteenth century-ish).

The *caravanserai* was a trading center/self-service hotel/café/marketplace/mini-fortress/stables/watering hole. Traveling at the time wasn't that safe, and merchants often carried very precious cargos; these establishments were thus often to be found just 30 miles apart (i.e., one day's camel ride). Travelers could cook their own food in the shared cauldron, feed their animals, buy and sell stuff, fill up their water bottles, sleep, and chat.

Just one thing: the *caravanserai* thing is not actually a thing of the past. The word is still very much in use in Iran, and my husband has fond memories of traveling with his parents when he was a child and visiting such establishments for wayside refreshment and cheap overnight lodgings. Wouldn't it be fun to set up a chain of them along our famously bandit-ridden highways?

Manti

KAZAKH DUMPLINGS

Mmmm. Dumplings. This is another recipe with decidedly Far Eastern overtones: it is most likely that the dish was first created by the Uighurs in Western China, and traveled (perhaps with that enterprising guy Ghengis Khan, who spread culture and terror in equal measure) west to Central Asia. The Turkic nations also seem mighty fond of it, which is why it crops up in Turkey and Armenia. The original ingredients almost certainly comprised horsemeat, which remains popular in the region, but as we live in a nation of hippophiles and in the interests of keeping my store windows intact, I have substituted lamb.

MAKES ABOUT 24

FOR THE PASTA:
scant 3 cups/14oz/400g all-purpose flour
1 level tsp salt
¾ cup/175ml cold water

FOR THE FILLING:
14oz/400g coarsely ground lamb
1 onion, grated
2 green chilies, finely chopped
1 bunch of fresh cilantro, chopped
1 level tsp ground cumin
salt and freshly ground black pepper
3½ tbsp/1¾ oz/50g butter, cut into 24 cubes

Sift the flour and salt into a mixing bowl and trickle in the water, mixing with a wooden spoon, to form a stiff dough. Knead it with your hands for 5–10 minutes, then roll it into a ball, cover with a damp cloth, and let it rest for an hour. You may do the same if you wish.

To make the filling, squish the lamb together with all the other ingredients apart from the butter, pounding well so that the heat from your hands "warms" the fat of the lamb (this will help the flavors to mingle better).

When you are ready to cook the *manti*, scatter some flour on your work surface, divide the dough into 2 balls, roll each one out into an oblong about 1⅙in/2mm thick, then use a circular pastry cutter (3¼in/8cm in diameter is ideal, or you can improvise with a jar lid). Put a dollop of the meat mixture on one side of each one, dot it with a lump of butter, and fold the other semi-circle over to form a pocket. Crimp the edges loosely with your fingers to seal the *manti*.

Quarter-fill a steamer with water and bring it to a boil on the stovetop. If you do not have a patent steaming device, all is not lost: you can improvise with a lidded colander (or stack of them) set over a pan of boiling water. Grease the parts of the basket (or colander), which will come into contact with the dough, and carefully arrange the dumplings inside. If your steamer has only one layer, then you will need to cook the *manti* in 2–3 batches. Steam them for about 40 minutes, and serve hot or cold with yogurt* or chili sauce.

* BONUS RECIPE: QUICK YOGURT SAUCE
Mix about 7oz/200g plain yogurt with 5–6 minced garlic cloves, 5 tbsp/75ml cold water plus salt and freshly ground black pepper to taste. Add 1 tbsp chopped dill (optional). Couldn't really be any simpler.

THE NORTH-EASTERN FRONTIER: YOUR CUT-OUT-AND-KEEP GUIDE TO CENTRAL ASIA

Let's face it—very few of us know anything about the five nations that make up the north eastern front of Snackistan. We know Ghengis Khan and Borat: hard to say which did the most damage to the region, but please let's forget about the latter. We're talking about the countries of the western steppes: vast and wild, a beguiling blend of Middle Eastern culture with the perceived (and totally fictitious) romance of the horsemen invaders from the north.

It is tempting to lump them all together: they are all former states of the Soviet Union, and all acquired their independence at the same time (around 1991). In fact, they have been tugged at and bickered over for millennia: the Mongols, the Moghuls, the Achaemenids, Alexander—they've all tried running the place. The Russians and Brits even had a word for the struggle to govern it: the Great Game. The area has also been known as Greater Khorassan and Transoxiana (my favorite): Central Asia is perhaps more apt. The five countries are in the process of forming a Central Asian Union, which may promote economic stability in the region. They are collectively an averred nuclear-free zone. More relevant to the context of our book is the fact that their cuisine is all very similar, with rice and wheat at its core. They are all also inordinately fond of meat. Ho hum.

And yet there are huge variations: the landscape varies from mountains to deserts to steppe, and the people are partly Turkic, partly Persian. Turkmenistan and Kazakhstan are kind of thriving, while the other three are impoverished and not entirely stable. Anyway, because I am totally fascinated by the area, here's a very abbreviated country-by-country summary of what I think you should know.

...KAZAKHSTAN: is the ninth largest country in the world, and, astonishingly for such a vast area, it is completely landlocked. It has a varied climate and terrain and is well endowed on the natural resources front. Which might explain why it is so prosperous. The capital is Astana, and the people are mostly Turkic, descended from Turkic and Mongol nomads. It grows lots and lots of wheat, and is thought to be the country whence the apple originated. On to...

...KYRGYZSTAN: this is a very poor land, with a largely rural economy and huge civil unrest: as I type, there is a state of virtual anarchy in the capital Bishkek. The country is rich in minerals, but has little natural fuel of its own. And it is something like 80 percent mountains, which makes it very photogenic but hard to farm and govern. The people were originally Indo-European, but there is strong Turkic influence too, while the official language is still Russian. The *Epic of Manas* tells the story of the eponymous national hero and his 40 tribes of descendants: a popular pastime is to listen to the Manaschis, storytellers who recount his great deeds. Kyrgyzstan's other favorite hobby is *Ulak Tartysh* (known elsewhere as *buzkashi*), where dashing young men wrestle on horseback for the headless carcass of a goat. Right on. The habit in my own home town of climbing a slippery pole to acquire a stuck pig is clearly so much more sensible. Next stop…

…TAJIKISTAN: another very mountainous country—it has the Pamir range running right through its middle. And another poor nation; sadly, its chief export is cheap labor, as large numbers of its young men are becoming economic migrants, sending money home for their families. Drugs are an issue, both the production and usage. It does produce decent quantities of cotton and rare metals, but is still in a state of depression after a civil war in the 1990s. It is hoped that the completion of the Anzab Tunnel through the mountains will bring new prosperity to the country and the capital, Dushanbe: this is part of a new transport corridor that pundits have tagged the New Silk Route. Tajikistanis are of similar descent to the Persians, and remain close to Iran. If it's Tuesday it must be…

…TURKMENISTAN: a thriving land, albeit notoriously corrupt. Most of the land mass is as flat as *barberi* bread: it is 80 percent desert in fact. But Turkmenistan is extremely rich in natural resources, boasting both gas and oil. And it has a coast, which is always a helpful accessory for a country. Its other main product is cotton, although it is also famed for its melons. The nation was ravaged by the actions of invaders through the centuries, especially that arch-vandal Ghengis Khan. But the ancient capital Nisa can still be seen today, near the modern capital Ashgabat. The national drink, apart from the ubiquitous green tea, is *chal*, which is made from fermented camel milk. Which is probably better than it sounds. Last stop is…

…UZBEKISTAN: this is where you will find Samarkand and Bukhara and Chashkand (now Tashkent, the modern capital), just the names of which resonate with faraway fantasy. The Uzbeks are largely Turkic, as is their language, although the ancient residents were actually Scythians. The country is not now very well off, although it benefited like no other from the Silk Route trade. It has been particularly badly hit by the all but disappearance of the Aral Sea (which was triggered when the Russians decided to jack the water it contained). Useless piece of info about Uzbekistan: it is one of just two countries in the world that are doubly landlocked i.e., surrounded by countries that are themselves landlocked.

That's it—hope you've enjoyed your tour. Please fly with us again.

Çörek

TURKISH MILK BREAD WITH SESAME

Most countries have a version of this: a soft, glazed, egg-enriched bread, a bit like brioche, or *challah*, or what in Iran is known as *naan sheermal*. Now I am a self-confessed butter glutton, but this stuff is really rather cakey, and pretty addictive all on its own. It is also a great dunker: try it with coffee, or chocolate, or just with warm spiced milk...

In Turkey, *çörek* is most often to be found starring in a breakfast role: it can be made as a savory roll, or, as here, a sweet, seeded braid.

SATES 4–6

1 envelope (¼ oz/7g) active dry yeast
   (or ½ oz/14g fresh)
²/₃ cup/150ml warm milk
½ cup/3½ oz/100g sugar
scant 3¼ cups/1lb/450g all-purpose flour
½ tsp salt
1 level tsp ground cinnamon
2 eggs, beaten

10½ tbsp/5½ oz/150g butter, softened

FOR THE GLAZE/TOPPING:

¼ tsp ground saffron dissolved in
   1 tbsp boiling water
1 egg, beaten
2 tbsp hulled sesame seeds
2 tsp nigella seeds

Dissolve the yeast in the warm milk together with 1¾oz/50g of the sugar, and set it aside for 10 minutes to do its thing.

Sift the rest of the sugar into a bowl together with the flour, salt, and cinnamon and make a well in the middle. Whisk the eggs and butter together then pour them into the well along with the yeast mixture. Stir it all together with a wooden spoon, then knead with your hands until it comes together (if it looks dry, add a little cold water). Cover the bowl and leave the dough somewhere warm to rise for around 2 hours.

After 2 hours, knead the dough on a lightly floured surface for around 5 minutes more then split it into 6 or 8 lumps as required. Stretch two of these into strips of 6–8in/15–20cm and pinch them together at one end before twisting them into a loose braid. Repeat with the other pairs of strips, then leave the dough to rise again for another 15 minutes.

Sprinkle the saffron into a tablespoonful of boiling water and set it aside to cool. Meanwhile, preheat the oven to 375°F/190°C.

When the saffron water has cooled a little, whisk it into the egg and use a pastry brush or a wad of paper towel to spread the glaze over the *çörek*. Sprinkle the seeds over the braids, then put them on to a greased baking tray and bake for around 25 minutes, or until they are a dark golden-brown color. Enjoy warm or cold: if you store them wrapped in plastic or in an airtight plastic tub, they will keep for 4–5 days.

Tashreeb

IRAQI BREAD STEW

The word *tashreeb* is derived from *sharab*, which means both "a drink," and "wine." In this context, it refers to bread "drinking up" the juices from cooked meat and vegetables: it is in fact applied to a whole range of dishes that are cooked on or served over stale bread. In Snackistan, a lot of snacks are made from recycled leftovers, which is a laudable state of affairs; as a shopkeeper, I am fairly well qualified to rant about the culinary *zeitgeist* of the nation, and I can tell you that in the West we are wasteful and far too obsessed with best-before dates.

This is perfect weekday supper food: thrifty, comforting, filling, and mostly one-pot-fare. Once you've mastered these two recipes (said the food writer, patronizingly), play around with the concept yourself. Cook a whole chicken inside a large *khobez*, or use stale French bread slices (and let's face it, French bread goes stale after about three hours) to support cheesy baked mushrooms—there's a whole new -istan of possibilities there.

SUPPER FOR 4 (WITH LAMB)

2 large onions, chopped

dash of oil, for frying

1lb 2oz/500g boneless shoulder of lamb, cut into small pieces

1 tsp ground turmeric

1 tsp *baharat* (Iraqi seven spice mix—substitute pumpkin pie spice with added cumin, coriander, and black pepper if you can't find the real deal)

½ tsp ground black pepper

1 tbsp tomato paste

1 can (14oz/400g) chopped tomatoes

4 dried black limes (known as *noomi*—they are readily available in Middle Eastern stores, but if you cannot find them just drop ½ a fresh lemon in instead)

salt, to taste

3–4 stale pita breads, or 1–2 *khobez* (or any other dry old bread)

Fry the onions in a little oil, adding the chopped lamb once they have softened. Cook the lamb until it is sealed, then add the spices, stirring well, followed a minute or so later by the tomato paste and tomatoes. Add around ⅔ cup/150ml water and bring the contents of the pan to a gentle boil.

Next, rinse the dried limes, prick them with a fork, and drop them into the sauce. Cover the pan and simmer for around 1½ hours, or until the lamb is soft, really soft. Finally, add salt to taste.

If your bread is still soft, bake it or fry it for a few minutes to crisp it up, then pull or cut it into rough pieces before spreading it out over the base of a casserole/serving dish. Ladle the lamb and stock on top, and serve with thick plain yogurt or the *Borani-ye-bademjun* on p.118.

ALTERNATIVE VEGGIE VERSION:

ALSO SERVES 4

pure (non-extra-virgin) oil, for frying

2 large onions, chopped

2 green bell peppers, cut into
    long fat strips

3 sticks of celery, cut into
    1½–2in/4–5cm chunks

¾ in/2cm piece fresh ginger,
    peeled and minced

2 garlic cloves, chopped

2–3 green chili peppers, chopped (optional)

1 large eggplant, cut into
    1¼ in/3cm chunks

1 fat zucchini, cut into
    1¼ in/3cm chunks

4 large tomatoes

1 tbsp tomato paste

1 level tsp dried oregano

1 level tsp dried thyme

generous ¾ cup/200ml cold water

salt and freshly ground black pepper

3–4 whole-wheat pita breads
    (or equivalent other bread)

1 pack halloumi, cut into
    1/16–⅛ in/2–3mm slices

big handful of fresh parsley, chopped

Preheat the oven to 375°F/190°C.

Heat a glug of oil in a pan and fry the onions, peppers, and celery until they are soft. Next, add the ginger, garlic, and chili, stirring well, followed by the eggplant, zucchini, and tomato. After a few minutes, add the tomato paste, herbs, and water, bring the whole thing to a boil, season to taste, turn down the heat, and simmer for around 30 minutes.

Grease an ovenproof dish and warm in the oven. Toast the pitas until they puff up, then open them up. Fill the pockets with halloumi slices, then cut each pita into pieces before arranging them in the bottom of the oven dish. Pour the bubbling vegetables on top, cover with foil, and bake for around 30 minutes. Strew with the parsley and serve hot with yogurt and maybe some extra bread for dunking.

THE SNACKISTAN SANDWICH BAR

The Earl of Sandwich has to be one of the world's most famous eponymous dudes. Surely over half of the Western world's working population call upon his name every lunchtime. He undoubtedly introduced this ultimate snack to the West with his call for a repast of beef served between two slices of bread to obviate the need to interrupt a particularly good session of cards. But he most certainly wasn't the first hungry guy to resort to a quick bite of stuff wrapped in bread. Card players and other hungry peops have been doing so for thousands of years, and there is ample evidence to suggest that the practice started in the Middle East. Wheat cultivation and farming in general evolved in the area now covered by northwest Iran and eastern Iraq, and the first breads are believed to have been made (possibly as a by-product of beer) in ancient Egypt. The first recorded instance of sandwich-building is in all likelihood that of the great Jewish leader Hillel, who during the Passover Seder "sandwiched" bitter herbs between two sheets of bread by way of repenting of past misdeeds. The business of using bread as a plate for food was common in the Middle Ages, and both Greeks and Turks have been making pita bread sammies for centuries.

Thus Snackistan has a rich history of exotic sandwiches on which to draw. I have but highlighted the ones I find most interesting...

FALAFEL POCKET: THE DEFINITIVE MIDDLE-EASTERN SANDWICH

Falafel. They were probably created in Egypt, made the Levant their spiritual home, and have now conquered the world. And they are about the only veggie option for late-night munchies (although there is always a slice of cheese). When they are fresh, moist, and perfectly cooked, they are a delight. If they are dry or overcooked, frankly I wouldn't even give them to Master Shopcat.

To make the perfect falafel sammie, apart from perfect falafel you also need the perfect extras: piquant sauce, fresh salad, pert pickles, and crisp but not too crisp bread. If you are at home, it is rather fun to re-create that greasy vegan spoon experience by putting a range of possible fillings out and inviting people to build their own sandwiches. In fact, you could even cook the falafel at the table, like a fondue—although that might be a bit messy/dangerous.

PER PERSON:
1 pita bread (whole wheat is tastier, really)
3 hot fresh falafel (store-bought or see below)

OPTIONAL EXTRAS:
Patent Snackistan Kebab Salad Mix (p.63)
tahini (see p.158—you'll need about 2 tbsp per person)
extra special chili sauce (see right—again, about 2 tbsp per person)

Avocado and Yogurt Dip with Sumac (p.128)
houmous (see p.120)
grilled halloumi
fried baby cauliflower florets
fried eggplant slices
fried potatoes (aka french fries)
fried beet chips
pickled cucumbers or mixed pickle (see p.10 or 12)
lemon wedges

BONUS RECIPE: EXTRA-SPECIAL CHILI SAUCE

If you're a bit of a kebab head, or enjoy this sort of snack on a regular basis, keeping a bottle of this homemade chili sauce in the fridge is a fine idea. Fry 2 medium chopped onions with 5–6 chopped garlic cloves, 2 chopped Scotch bonnet or Habanero chilies (or 6–7 green chilies), 1 diced green bell pepper, and 2 chopped sticks of celery. When soft, add 1 tsp ground coriander, ½ tsp cinnamon, ½ tsp cumin, and 1 heaped tsp tomato paste. Stir well for a few minutes, then add 2 cans (14oz/400g) chopped tomatoes, and 4 tbsp pomegranate molasses. Simmer for about 10 minutes, season to taste, blend, cool, and bottle in sterilized jars (see p.10) until needed.

The only secret with this falafel banquet is to serve all the hot stuff hot. So get it all ready, and keep it warm until needed.

FALAFEL REFRESHER COURSE

What? You want to know how to make falafel as well? Oh—alright then. To make about 15: soak scant 1 cup/5½oz/150g each of dried chickpeas and dried split fava beans (or just use chickpeas) in water overnight. Drain and blend with ½ teaspoon each baking soda and chili powder, and 1 teaspoon ground cumin, ½ bunch each of chopped parsley and cilantro, 1 large onion, 4–5 garlic cloves, and salt to taste. If the mixture's too wet, add flour; if too dry, add water. Form into balls and deep-fry until they are golden brown and float on the surface. Drain on paper towel. Done.

Sabich

VEGGIE DAGWOOD SANDWICH

This is my kind of sandwich: maximalist. It contains a whole pantry of potential *mezze* items in one pita pocket, creating one unfeasibly fat bite.

The ingredients for the filling of *sabich* were actually staple Sabbath fare for Iraqi Jews, many of whom entered Israel in the 1940s and 1950s. Israeli street vendors soon turned the combo into a sandwich, and it now gives the falafel pocket a run for its shekels as the nation's favorite street food. I think of it as an eggplant sandwich, but it also contains potato, egg, pickled cucumbers, mango pickle, tomato and cucumber salad, fresh herbs, *houmous*, and *tahini*. The somewhat anomalous mango pickle (*ambeh*) insinuated its way into *sabich* after voyaging from India to Iraq c/o silk route traders.

If I am making it for a few people at home, I like to serve *sabich* as a *mezze* spread, putting all the ingredients in little bowls and letting folk create their own: there is something very appealing about self-assembly food.

✱ Note on tahini

Ah, *tahini*. Well *tahina* as you buy it, is famous for its cement-like texture. In order to render it into *tahini* "sauce," you need to blend it with lemon juice, water, salt, and freshly ground black pepper until it becomes pale and creamy and much more workable. It thickens in the fridge, so it is a good idea to make it a little runnier than you require. Add garlic, cilantro, and parsley as well, and you have a lovely hearty dip that the Cypriots call *tashi*.

SERVES 4

salt

1 large eggplant, thinly sliced

2 medium waxy potatoes, scrubbed and
    sliced into 1/16 in/2mm rounds

oil, for frying

2 garlic cloves, sliced

2 medium tomatoes, diced

1/2 cucumber, finely diced

1 small onion, finely diced

1/2 bunch of fresh parsley, chopped

1/2 bunch of fresh cilantro, chopped

juice and grated zest of 1 lemon

ground black pepper

4 slices pita bread (whole wheat is better
    for you, and tastier. Just saying...)

2 tbsp *houmous* (see p.120)

2 tbsp *tahini**

4 perfectly hard-boiled eggs, sliced

2 tbsp salty mango pickle

8 sliced pickled cucumbers (see p.12)

Sprinkle some salt on the eggplant slices and set aside: the salt draws the moisture and innate bitterness from the vegetable. After around 20 minutes, dab them with paper towel.

Fry the potatoes in a splash of oil until they are soft and golden-ish (or you can boil them until they are just cooked: this would be healthier and more authentic). Remove them with a slotted spoon and drain them on paper towel; then fry the garlic and eggplants in the same oil, adding more if necessary, again removing them with a slotted spoon to drain.

Mix the tomato, cucumber, onion, herbs, lemon juice, zest, pepper, and some salt together.

Preheat the grill, if using. Grill or toast the pita until it puffs up, then split it along one side to create a fillable pocket. Spread one side of the cavity of each with *houmous* and the other with *tahini*. Next, add a couple of slices of the fried eggplant and potato to each, then top these with sliced egg. Spoon some mango pickle over the egg, followed with the pickled cucumbers. Top with the salady salsa. I recommend that you eat it immediately.

Hawawshi

EGYPTIAN MEAT POCKETS

SERVES 2

10½ oz/300g ground beef (fatty
　works best)

1 small–medium onion, grated

1–2 garlic cloves, minced

1 large tomato, diced

1 green chili, diced

1 level tsp ground cumin

1 level tsp dried mint

handful of fresh parsley, chopped

½ tsp salt

1 large *khobez* (or 2 small pita
　breads), whole-wheat if
　possible as it is tastier and
　better for you

olive oil

1–2 tsp *dukka* (optional topping;
　see p.20)

TO SERVE:

liquid *labneh* (lightly salted thick
　Greek yogurt will also do) or
　tahini (see p.158)

Now this is fun, albeit counter-kitchen-intuitive. An Egyptian *enchilada*, made with raw ground meat, which is then baked inside the bread. It is of course amazingly tasty, as all the dripping goodness from the meat gets soaked up by the bread. My Egyptian customers tell me that this street snack is especially popular in Alexandria. And who am I to argue?

Everyday bread in Egypt is known as *aish*, and comes in two main varieties: *aish shamsi* (made with white flour) and *aish baladi* (made with whole wheat). It is to all intents and purposes the same as the *khobez* or pita that is now so easily available in the West, and so that is what we will use.

Preheat the oven to 375°F/190°C.

Mix the meat with the diced vegetables, chili, cumin, herbs, and salt. Pound it for a good few minutes: the warmth of your hands will soften the fat content of the meat and help the flavors mingle.

Cut the bread in half to form two semicircles, then split each half open to form two pockets. Smear the meat mixture across the bottom layer of each pocket and press the pockets a little so that they "close." Brush the outside of the bread with a drop of oil, and sprinkle some *dukka* on top if you have some handy.

Now wrap the *hawawshi* in parchment paper and plop them on a baking tray. Bake for about 15 minutes, then turn the sandwiches over and bake for a further 15 minutes, or until the bread is crispy and the meat sizzling.

Serve with a drizzle of *labneh* or *tahini* sauce. They are astonishingly wholesome.

PERSIAN-STYLE HERB WRAP

SERVES 1

a handful of flatbread (*lavash* or
　village bread: the kind that
　you don't need to heat)

labneh or cream cheese
　(my addition: I am not a
　hardcore herbivore like
　Mr. Shopkeeper)

a handful of herbs or salad leaves

This simple Persian fare is my simple* Persian husband's third favorite snackette. See, we always keep a big basket of herbs at home (of which more in the note on p.162). So if he's in a big hurry, or my wifely failings have left a slight hiatus in the snack provisions department, he will gorge on this. It is surprisingly satisfying, and obviously much healthier than his first favorite snackette (which consists of most of Chapter Three). Its other great virtue is that it takes about three seconds to assemble.

*Simple in tastes, only. Let it be known that in every other respect he is far cleverer than I.

Rip off a strip of bread. Smear it with *labneh*. Grab a handful of herbs and wrap the bread around it. End of story.

Sarnweech-e-Zaban
IRANIAN TONGUE SANDWICH

SERVES 2

2 small baguettes

6 Iranian-style pickled
    cucumbers (see p.12),
    finely sliced lengthways

2 nice tomatoes, finely sliced

big handful of fresh parsley and
    cilantro, chopped

small handful of shredded lettuce

2 cooked lambs' tongues, sliced

salt and freshly ground black
    pepper

2 lemon wedges

A note on herbs

OK: now about those herbs. Travelers to *Persia in Peckham* and *The New Middle Eastern Vegetarian* will have heard me enthuse about the wonders of Persian herb consumption. Most Iranian households keep a big basket of washed and sorted *sabzi khordan* (literally: herbs for eating) in their fridge: these make an appearance at lunch and dinner, as great handfuls of herbs are eaten as an appetizer and an aid to digestion. The selection usually comprises fresh parsley, mint, cilantro, basil, cress, chives, and tarragon, along with scallions and radishes. It is also very handy to keep such a resource for cooking purposes: we could all do with eating (and growing) more herbs. Washed herbs keep well in a colander or plastic bag in the fridge for around 5 days.

Offal is big in the Middle East. Nothing gets wasted—sheep feet, brains, and heads, sheep or calves liver, heart, and kidneys... and tongue. We do of course have a long history of eating tongue in the West, but it is not perhaps as widespread as it once was (yup—we are getting squeamish), and certainly not in the sphere of fast food.

Iranian sandwiches (which are rather sweetly known as *sarnweech*) are made with small French-style baguettes, and come in eight or nine popular varieties, all with the same accompaniments: they do not use sauce, or butter, or mayonnaise, so what you get is just meat and/or vegetable goodness. Tongue is the most popular; the *sarnweech-e-zaban* is practically a street-food institution.

Split the baguettes lengthways, line with the pickled cucumber, tomato, herbs, and lettuce. Sprinkle the tongue with salt and pepper and arrange it on top of the salad filling. Add lemon as required. And that's it.

HOW TO COOK A TONGUE

Lambs' tongues are readily available from good independent butchers. When you get them home, clean them as best you can, and put them in a pan with water, chopped celery, onion, bay leaves, black peppercorns, and a handful of chickpeas (which serve to absorb any "strong" cooking smells). Bring to a boil, turn down the heat, and simmer for 2–3 hours (more if you want to enjoy them as a casserole), keeping an eye on the liquid levels: add salt right at the end (adding it too soon makes the meat tough). Remove the tongue from the cooking stock and allow to cool a little before peeling off the outer skin. Chill well before slicing. If you have children at home, it is fun to leave the tongues really visible in the fridge: you will then be met with a barrage of "Eww! Gross!" as you snigger in the next room.

Halwah: Sweet Treats

Nasruddin was traveling on pilgrimage with two Sufis. Night was drawing in, and they had just enough money to pay for lodgings. The only food they had left between them was a little halva, and it was not enough to share. Unable to decide how to divide it, they decided to wait until morning: whoever recounted the best dream would be awarded the prize of a sweet breakfast.

In the morning, the first Sufi described how his hunger had driven him to see a great white light and how he had felt at utter peace. The second described how he had seen a plain of whirling dervishes, a sight so beautiful that he had cried out in his sleep.

They turned expectantly to the Mullah. "Well, my comrades, I cannot hope to match your reveries with my meagre tale." But his travel companions begged him to divulge it anyway. "I dreamed that I saw my original Sufi teacher, and that he said: 'Nasruddin—EAT THE HALVA NOW!' Of course I had no choice but to obey..."

Halva (or *halwah* in Arabic) is a great substance: it varies from village to village and is as easy to pin to one recipe as the original manna from heaven. To all intents and purposes, it means "sweetmeat": the stuff that we know and scarf as *halva* (a sesame and sugar confection) is but one (mostly Mediterranean) version, and in fact most are roux (i.e. flour and butter) based.

Sweets are eaten as snacks in Snackistan far more than they are eaten as desserts. Dessert is not a regular occurrence, but a sugary treat with tea is as natural to most Middle Easterners as milk and cookies are to the average American. And oh what a fabulous range of sweet eats from which they can choose: it goes from the very healthy, such as simple boiled fruit paste, through to the frankly evil indulgence that is baklava.

The following is a funny mishmash of authentic treats, street snacks, and uniquely Snackistani recipes.

Umm Ali

ALI'S MOTHER'S PUDDING

SERVES 6

around 12oz/350g (raw weight) frozen or chilled puff pastry (phyllo will do) or 4 large plain croissants (stale will do)

2 cups/450ml (or 1 can) condensed milk

generous 2 cups /500ml water

5–6 drops vanilla extract

¾ cup/3½ oz/100g unsweetened shredded coconut

1⅓ cups/7oz/200g mixed nuts: choose from slivered almonds, chopped pistachios, blanched, chopped hazelnuts, pine nuts, and chopped raw cashews

½ cup/125ml whipping cream, duly whipped

½ cup/1¾ oz/50g toasted flaked almonds or chopped pistachios, to decorate

This is one of Egypt's favorite childhood desserts. I just love food with a story attached. Such dishes become deeply ensconced in a nation's culinary heart. This Egyptian classic comes with one of the best ancient urban legends attached…

Many centuries ago (in around 1250 AD in fact, at the time of the Crusades), Egypt was left king-less when its Sultan of the time, al-Salih Ayyoub, contracted a fever suddenly and died. His resourceful wife, a former slave by the name of Shajjar al-Durr, took over and by all accounts was pretty good in her assumed role until the Caliph of Baghdad found out. He wasn't having a woman ruler on his watch, and so he sent a guy called Aybak to marry her and help around the house/kingdom.

Shajjar al-Durr quite liked her new husband, and prevailed upon him to divorce his first wife, who went by the name of Umm Ali (Ali's mother).

Things were fine for seven years, and then Shajjar al-Durr discovered that Aybak wasn't quite the catch she'd thought he was. And so she had him killed in the bath, as you did if you were a queen 750 years ago.

Word of this reached Umm Ali, and she decided that enough was enough. And so she arranged for the Sultana to be murdered in revenge. Shajjar al-Durr was beaten to death with clogs by her own maidservants, and Umm Ali devised a rich dessert by way of celebration: for with the Atabeg and Sultana out of the way, her own son Ali was surely in line for the throne. She arranged for the sweetmeat to be handed out in the streets of Cairo and it soon became popular fare. To this day, it is known by the name of its vengeful creator: Umm Ali, and it proves that revenge is a dish that can actually be eaten either hot or cold.

Preheat the oven to 400°F/200°C.

Bake the pastry according to the instructions on the package: this will usually involve greased baking trays, the preheated oven, and 15–20 minutes cooking time, or until the pastry has risen and is golden brown. Set aside, but leave the oven on as you'll need it again.

Stir the condensed milk, water, and vanilla together in a small saucepan and bring them gently to a boil. Turn down the heat and simmer for around 5 minutes. Take off the heat.

Cut the pastry into squares and assemble in a fairly large oven tray (8 x 13 x 1¼ in / 20 x 30 x 3cm is ideal). If you are using croissants instead (and I think they turn out better), just pull them apart roughly with your hands and spread them over the dish. Sprinkle the coconut and your chosen nut mixture over the pastry, then drizzle the condensed milk mixture over the top, taking care not to wash all the topping into one corner. Allow the milk to soak in for a few moments then spoon the whipped cream over the top.

Bake for around 15 minutes, or until the top is golden and set. Sprinkle with the nut decoration and scarf. This is best enjoyed hot (but not straight out of the oven as it is kind of burny-mouthy), but works well chilled for breakfast the next day.

THREE RECIPES FROM THE SNACKISTAN CAKE PAN...

Khobez Timur
DATE AND FIG BREAD

A hearty winter treat, and it's got fruit in it, so it must be good for you, yes? This is nice lightly toasted and slathered with butter or *labneh*, but it is pretty good just on its own as well. And obviously if you use a good-quality margarine instead of butter, this cake becomes vegan.

MAKES 1 LOAF (8–10 SLICES)

3½ oz/100g pitted dates (while Iranian Bam dates are the best in the world, slightly drier, stickier dates are better for cake-making), chopped

3½ oz/100g dried figs, chopped

1 cup/250ml very hot Earl Grey tea (strained)

scant 1 cup/6½ oz/180g soft dark brown sugar

9 tbsp/4½ oz/125g butter, softened

scant 3¼ cups/1lb/450g all-purpose flour (spelt works well too)

1 heaped tsp baking powder

1 tsp ground cardamom

1 tsp ground cinnamon

½ cup/2¾ oz/75g roughly chopped walnuts, plus 3–4 intact halves

Plop the dates and figs into the tea, then add the sugar. Leave for 10 minutes or so (to allow the fruit to soften and the sugar to dissolve), then add the butter, stirring so it melts in the still-warm water.

Preheat the oven to 350°F/180°C and line a standard 10 x 5 x 3 in/1kg loaf pan with parchment paper (or greased wax paper).

Sift the flour and baking powder into a bowl and add the spices and nuts. Beat in the soaked fruity mix. Spoon the mixture into the prepared pan, pressing it down so that it is evenly distributed. Push the intact walnuts into the top by way of decoration and bake for 45 minutes, or until it is firm to the touch (see Zucchini and Eggplant cake, opposite). Enjoy warm or cold: if kept wrapped, this cake will keep for up to a week.

ZUCCHINI AND EGGPLANT CAKE

I am truly the antithesis of a domestic goddess. In fact, until a few months ago, I had never made my husband a cake. I know: you're all shocked. There is probably some statute that proclaims that non-cake-making is a form of neglect. Anyway, he was naturally fairly excited that I had finally given in to my inner baking muse. But what did I produce for him? A sumptuous Victoria sponge? A fanciful fondant masterpiece? A manly fruitcake? Um, no, it was this: zucchini and eggplant loaf. Poor dear.

Notwithstanding my wifely failings, this is rather a good recipe, and just so very snackable. It should be pointed out that cakes, as in spongy, frosted, sandwiched, cut-into-wedges type things, are rare across Snackistan, and are quite often either African or Orthodox Christian in origin, thus from Greece, Turkey, Armenia, and Georgia. Having said that, incredibly ancient Babyonian tablets have been found which refer to a date-nutty-bread-cake thing called *mersu*. Anyway, this is inspired by something I once had in an Armenian café.

Preheat the oven to 400°F/200°C.

Prick the eggplant and bake for around 30 minutes, or until it is quite soft. Take out of the oven, cut open, and leave to cool.

Grate the zucchini and press it against a sieve to try and squeeze out some of its water content. Leave it to drain for 15 minutes, or so.

Next, break the eggs into your favorite cake-making bowl and beat in the sugar. Whisk vigorously for 2 minutes, although you won't be able to tell that the mixture is paling as the sugar is quite dark. Mix in the butter and oil, then beat in the dry ingredients and spices.

Once the eggplant is fairly cool, peel it carefully, retaining the skin, and finely chop the flesh. Press the grated zucchini against the sieve a little more to get any residual water out of the flesh, then add it to the cake mixture together with the chopped eggplant and nuts and seeds, stirring well.

Reheat the oven to 350°F/180°C. Grease a standard 10 x 5 x 3in/1kg loaf pan and line it with parchment paper or greased wax paper. Because grease is the word is the motion.

Carefully arrange the retained eggplant skin in the bottom of the prepared pan, then spoon the cake mixture on top, tapping the bottom of the pan so that the mixture levels itself out. Bake in the oven for around 45 minutes, then turn the oven down to 340°F/170°C and bake for another 20–25 minutes, or until the top of the cake feels firm. To check that it is cooked through, insert a metal skewer into the middle of the cake and withdraw it—if the tip is covered in wet-looking dough, you need to cook it for another 10 minutes or so. Leave to cool slightly before turning out and peeling away the paper.

Slice and serve warm or cold: it is pretty awesome with *labneh* (which is salted strained yogurt but tastes like cream cheese) spread on top. It will keep for a couple of days in an airtight container (and longer in the fridge), if you can leave it alone that long.

MAKES 1 LOAF
(8–10 SLICES)

1 eggplant

1 zucchini

2 large eggs

½ cup + 2 tbsp/4½ oz/125g sugar (use roughly half soft brown sugar and half superfine sugar)

5⅓ tbsp/2¾ oz/75g butter, melted (I use salted because I am a peasant)

scant ¼ cup/50ml good sunflower or canola oil

scant 1 cup/4½ oz/125g self-rising flour, sifted

½ tsp baking soda

1 tsp ground cinnamon

½ tsp ground mace (or nutmeg in a pinch)

1 tsp ground ginger

½ cup/1¾ oz/50g slivered almonds*

scant ½ cup/1¾ oz/50g pumpkin seeds*

* Nuts and seeds

You can use any other kinds you fancy: pistachios, walnuts, sunflower seeds, etc.

Yogurt Khavesi Tatlisi
TURKISH COFFEE AND YOGURT CAKE

Yogurt is pretty much ubiquitous in Turkish cuisine and (something like) this cake has been made in Turkey for centuries. Turkish coffee would more likely make an appearance as an accompaniment than an ingredient, but there is nothing stopping you from having one on the side as well, if you see what I mean. The cake is great on its own, but adding the syrup takes you pretty much to Snackistan nirvana (and also renders it dessert material as well as coffee-break fodder).

MAKES A REALLY BIG CAKE
(you'll need a 10in/25cm diameter round cake pan with a fixed base or equivalent-sized square pan)

FOR THE CAKE:
3 cups/14oz/400g self-rising flour
2 tsp baking powder
1 heaped tbsp finely ground Turkish coffee
    (or strong regular ground coffee in a pinch)
1 tsp ground cardamom
1 cup/250ml plain yogurt

generous ¾ cup/200ml honey
9 tbsp/4½ oz/125g salted butter, melted (or
    use oil and a pinch of salt)
3 eggs, beaten
1 tsp vanilla extract

FOR THE SYRUP:
1 cup/7oz/200g sugar
⅔ cup/150ml water
juice and grated zest of 1 orange
1 heaped tsp Turkish coffee (or strong regular
    ground coffee in a pinch)

On Yogurt

Well, the Turks are pretty sensible using as much of it as they do. Live probiotic yogurt aids the digestion and strengthens the gut. But you knew that already, yes? It is far more easily digestible than other dairy products, and so is often given to the sick or those with mild lactose intolerance. What you may not know is that it makes for one of the world's cheapest face masks (just slap it on all over, leave for 20 minutes, then wash it off again). And also that it can be the careless chef's best friend: in many commercial kitchens it is kept on hand as an instant soother for burns.

Preheat the oven to 350°F/180°C and line the cake pan with parchment paper.
Sift the first 4 ingredients into a bowl. Beat the remaining 5 cake ingredients together in another bowl, then introduce both sets of ingredients to each other, mixing well. Pour the cake mix into the prepared pan and bake for around 50 minutes, or until set on top and no longer gooey in the middle (see skewer trick on p.169).

Meanwhile, throw the syrup ingredients into a pan, bring to a gentle simmer, and bubble for around 10 minutes; then set aside to cool.

When the cake is cooked, turn out and baste with the orange-coffee syrup. This creation totally begs a generous dollop of crème fraîche (or to be authentic, *kaymak*) on the side. Enjoy warm or cold. Share if you must.

Lows Iyo Sisin

SOMALIAN-STYLE SESAME SNAPS

Scholars argue as to whether sesame seeds (*simsim* in Arabic) originated in Africa or India, but scholars are always disagreeing with each other, so let's just agree that they have been in the Middle East for thousands of years. Ancient Snackistanis clearly recognized how good they were as they accredited them with magic door-opening powers (remember Aladdin). They were traded in old Mesopotamia, and cultivated extensively by the Ancient Egyptians for uses ranging from cosmetic to medicinal. The seeds are undemanding little fellows, and grow well in desert-type conditions, so it is easy to understand how their usage became so widespread.

Sesame seeds contain protein, all manner of trace minerals, vitamin B, calcium, and tryptophan (which helps release serotonin, which makes you happy). The point being that this makes them practically perfect snack fodder.

They are strewn liberally across bread in countries all round the Mediterranean, and are of course the main component of both *tahina* and *halva*. In the Arabian Peninsula and East Africa, they are widely enjoyed in candy bar format: this is the best recipe I've found and comes from a consortium of my Somali customers.

MAKES AROUND 40 SQUARES, OR ENOUGH FOR A WEEK'S SNACKING

generous 1 cup/9oz/250g whole sesame seeds
1 cup/7oz/200g white sugar
¼ cup/3½ oz/100g honey
generous ½ cup/3½ oz/100g smooth peanut butter
scant ½ cup/100ml date syrup—if you can't find it, just use extra honey
¾ cup/3½ oz/100g unsweetened shredded coconut

Preheat the oven to 350°F/180°C.

Spread the sesame seeds out on a fairly large baking tray and put them into the oven for around 10 minutes, or until they assume a pleasant golden hue. Remove and set aside.

Tip, scrape, and dollop the sugar, honey, peanut butter, and date syrup into a saucepan and heat it through gently until the sugar has melted and everything has amalgamated.

Pour the toasted sesame seeds into the pan along with the coconut and mix thoroughly with a wooden spoon. Spread some oiled waxpaper over the baking tray, then spread the sesame gloop out over it, leveling it off with the wooden spoon. Place another sheet of waxpaper over the top: this will enable you to roll the gloop to a thickness of no more than about 1/16–1/8in/2–3mm; if necessary, use 2 trays. Now score through the sesame carefully, portioning it out into snack-sized squares. Leave to cool before breaking off the squares. Store in an airtight plastic container and dish out as rewards for very good behavior.

Badam Sokhteh

SAFFRON-SPICED CARAMELIZED ALMONDS

These are a very popular Iranian sweet, and oh-so-chewy: they offer perhaps the most likely explanation as to why so many Iranians train as dentists. Something like one in five dentists in my city (I've made up this statistic, but it can't be far wrong) are of Persian origin: they are clearly in cahoots with the confectionery manufacturers.

Versions of *badam sokhteh* are also made in Afghanistan and the lovely Claudia Roden refers to buying something similar in the Alexandria of her childhood.

MAKES JUST ENOUGH
1⅓ cups/7oz/200g shelled almonds (cashews would also respond well to this treatment)
1 cup/7oz/200g superfine sugar
½ tsp ground saffron steeped in a splash of boiling water
½ tsp ground cardamom
1 level tsp ground ginger
½ tsp salt

Preheat the oven to 340°F/170°C.

Spread the almonds out on a baking tray and roast them at for around 10 minutes, or until they have turned a more golden shade of brown.

Next, melt the sugar in a small saucepan, taking care not to let it boil. Once it has liquefied, add the saffron water, spices, and salt, stirring well; then take it off the heat and tip the roasted almonds in. Now brush a non-stick baking tray with a little oil and spread the almond mixture across it. Cover with a sheet of parchment paper or some such to keep flying things off it, and set somewhere cool until it hardens.

Break into snackable pieces and store in an airtight cookie jar or tin: *badam sokhteh* will keep for a few days before becoming soft.

ON DATES

It is impossible to overstate the importance of dates in Snackistan. They must have seemed like the original snack, after all; growing in the most unlikely and hostile of conditions and offering a practically perfect shot of nutrients to fortify weary desert travelers.

They have been around since Neolithic times, and are referred to in the *Epic of Gilgamesh*, the *Egyptian Book of the Dead*, the Bible, and the Koran. In the latter, they are often cited as an example of Allah's munificence; in one passage God sends them as a divine snack for the heavily pregnant Maryam (that's Mary):

Thereupon she conceived, and retired to a far-off place. And when she felt the pangs of childbirth she lay down by the trunk of a palm tree, crying: "O, would that I had died and passed into oblivion."

But a voice from above cried out to her: "Do not despair. Your Lord has provided a brook which runs at your feet, and if you shake the trunk of this palm tree it will drop fresh ripe dates into your lap. Therefore rejoice. Eat and drink."

In ancient times dates were credited with a seriously loopy list of health benefits, but they are undeniably a superfood, packing a punch of slow-release sugars, trace minerals, antioxidants, and vitamin B. They are also reputedly pretty good for the old libido…

We grow to the sound of the wind
Playing his flutes in our hair,
Palm tree daughters,
Brown flesh Badawi,
Fed with light
By our gold father;
We are loved of the free tented,
The sons of space, the
hall forgetters…
  E. P. Mathers, *The 1001 Nights*

Ranginak
IRANIAN DATE "SQUARES"

This is a classic Persian munchie, enjoyed especially during Ramadan or at times of religious significance: it is perfect for sharing, see, and it is not unusual for housewives to prepare huge trays to take to share out at the mosque. Its origins lie in the opulent court kitchens of Shiraz, however, and it can hold its own among the most lah-di-dah array of petits fours. *Ranginak* means "colorful," and once these are all decorated they do indeed look real pretty.

Pour the oil into a pan and heat it through: then stir in the flour and cook it until it becomes quite biscuity. Take it off the heat and add the sugar, cardamom, and half the cinnamon. Push a walnut half (or almond) into each date.

Now spread half the sweet roux mix out on a baking tray (one equating to 10 x 10in/ 25 x 25cm should do the trick). Layer the stuffed dates on top, then press the rest of the flour mixture on top to form a smooth surface. Sprinkle the top with the ground pistachios and the rest of the cinnamon, and put the tray into the fridge to chill. Once it is quite cold and firm, cut the *ranginak* into diamond shapes and serve with hot tea. They will keep in an airtight container for up to a week.

MAKES AROUND 30
1 cup/250ml oil (sunflower or
   canola)
3½ cups/1lb 2oz/500g
   all-purpose flour (whole
   wheat is also good here,
   although not authentic)
½ cup + 2 tbsp/4½ oz/125g
   superfine sugar
1 tsp ground cardamom
2 tbsp ground cinnamon
1¼ cups/4½ oz/125g walnut
   halves (or whole almonds)
1lb 2oz/500g pitted Bam (or
   other) dates
1½ tbsp ground shelled
   pistachios

Dibs W'rashi
DATE SYRUP FONDUE WITH *TAHINA*

COMFORT FOOD FOR 4

2 tbsp water

2 tbsp sugar

1 tsp orange blossom water

juice and grated zest of 1 orange

scant ½ cup/100ml date syrup

5 tbsp *tahina*

chunks of fruit for dipping:
strawberries, quarters of fig,
banana, pear, and apple slices,
mandarin segments, fat grapes

Dibs W'rashi is staple fare for much of Snackistan: it is eaten with bread for breakfast or as an any-time snack and is full of nutritious stuff. *Dibs* just means syrup, and in Turkey (where it is known as *pekmez*) the dish is often made with grape or mulberry syrup instead. Pomegranate molasses also works well.

Date syrup is special: it is creamy and has a caramel quality to it that belies its healthy and entirely natural origins. It can be used as a sweetener for pretty much any purpose, and also works well in savory dishes. The best stuff comes from Basra in Iraq, which is where this combo originated.

To make the basic spread, just mix five parts date syrup to one part *tahina*, add a squeeze of lemon juice, and spread on warm bread or toast. But just for fun I decided to turn this whole thing into a fondue.

Put the water, sugar, orange blossom water, and orange into a little pan and bring to a boil. Bubble for 5 minutes, then take off the heat, and stir in the date syrup and *tahina*. Either serve straight away or pour into your very retro 1970s-style fondue pot and keep warm until needed. Arrange the fruit bits prettily on your favorite retro party platter, and dive in.

Yakh Dar Behesht
PERSIAN ANGEL DELIGHT, KIND OF

COMFORT PUDDING FOR 6

generous ½ cup/2¾ oz/75g wheat starch (or cornstarch if you can't find it)

generous 2 cups/500ml water

generous ⅓ cup/1¾ oz/50g rice flour

generous 2 cups/500ml milk (use soy or rice milk if you like)

1¼ cups/9oz/250g sugar

5 tbsp rosewater

1 tsp ground cinnamon

1 tbsp chopped pistachios

Yakh dar behesht literally means "ice from heaven." This is a bit of a puzzle to me, because this light, rose-scented creation is not usually frozen at all: it is served more like a mousse, and its custardy texture means that it also works well as a layer in sweet flans or trifle.* I base my recipe on the late Roza Montazemi's version. Who is she? Kind of like a modern Iranian Mrs. Beeton. And she wrote what is possibly the biggest cookbook ever—*Honar-e-Ashpazi*.

Mix the starch with the water, then in a separate jug blend the rice flour with the milk. Pour both liquids into a heavy-bottomed pan and heat gently with the sugar and the rosewater. Bring to a boil, then turn down the heat and simmer until it thickens before pouring into a basin or individual glasses. Chill, decorate with the cinnamon and nuts, and serve.

*BONUS RECIPE: A trifling matter to prepare: soak some cake/croissants/baklava in strong Arabic or Greek coffee (with added rum if you like that sort of thing). Layer the resultant gloop into a trifle bowl (or individual dishes). Top with *yakh dar behesht* mix, make it pretty, chill, and there you have it—Snackistani trifle.

A QUARTET OF SP-ICE POPS

I would love to tell you that when my stepchildren were younger I regularly created homemade ice pops for them as they happily played in our perfectly manicured backyard. But I am totally not that organized, our kitchen is imploding, and our yard is a disgrace. These, then, have in part been created for Lewis, for I am now a wicked stepgrandmother: I will never be organized, but the kitchen might be done by the time he's five, and the garden is getting there. You can have too much halcyon anyway.

Ice pops, popsicles, call them what you will—they are so easy to make, and even easier to eat. I rarely bother with proper popsicle molds, but rather improvise with little pots—rinsed-out yogurt pots work well. DO NOT, however, do as I did during recipe testing and improvise with a nail file for a popsicle stick: this was not a good thing, no sirree. If you haven't got proper popsicle sticks, cut-down wooden skewers work well.

If you have the time and space, make two or three of the recipes below and overleaf: partly fill your molds with one, freeze them, then add a layer of another mixture, and so on. Call them traffic lights, or Snacksicles (occasionally, just occasionally, Americans have better words for stuff than we Brits do), or what you will—no one can deny that they look funky and you will earn yourself tons more awesome stepgrandma points.

Each recipe makes around 10–12 pops. Most homemade ice pops are best eaten sooner rather than later: a week or so is the norm.

CARDAMOM COFFEE

MAKES 10–12 POPS

generous 2 cups/500ml strong
    Arabic coffee with cardamom
    (you can buy it already
    blended, but if you prefer
    just make strong regular
    coffee with 4–5 crushed
    cardamom pods)*
1 cup/9oz/250g
    condensed milk

* You could use 2 cups/450ml coffee and scant ¼ cup/50ml rum. Just saying…

Are you a kitchen bowl-licker? This recipe is worth making for the privilege thereof alone. Condensed milk. No need to say any more, right? Obviously if you are giving it to small folk, decaf might be a better option.

Cool the coffee to room temperature, blend with the condensed milk, pour into popsicle molds (improvised or otherwise) and freeze. If you are using unofficial molds, don't forget to shove the popsicle sticks in after an hour or so.

SAFFRON, PISTACHIO, AND ROSEWATER CREAM

generous ¾ cup/200ml milk
⅓ tsp ground saffron
generous 1 cup/9oz/250g
    condensed milk
generous ¾ cup /200ml
    heavy cream
½ cup/2¾ oz/75g shelled
    pistachios
5 tbsp rosewater

Three of Iran's most bragged-about products all together in one frozen snack: it is an absolute classic.

Bring the milk just to boiling point in a heavy-bottomed pan and add the saffron. Allow it to steep for a few minutes before adding the condensed milk and cream. Gently bring it all to a boil, turn down the heat, and simmer briefly, stirring well, before taking off the heat.

Coarsely chop the pistachios: you are aiming for something finer than a sliver, but chunkier than ground nuts. Add them to the saffron cream along with the rosewater and set to chill somewhere.

When the mixture is quite cool, pour it into your chosen popsicle molds and freeze. Stir after an hour or so that the pistachio is evenly distributed.

FENNEL, MINT, AND GREEN TEA

3–4 tsp green tea leaves
4 tsp fennel seeds, crushed
3 cups/700ml water
big handful of fresh mint,
    chopped
6–7 tsp sugar

Antioxidizing and an aid to digestion: this is more than just your average ice pop, I'm telling you. All the ingredients are measured in teaspoons because that is surely the only way to measure tea.

Add the tea leaves and crushed fennel to the water in a very clean saucepan and bring to a boil. Turn down the heat and simmer for 3–4 minutes. Take off the heat, strain, then add the mint and sugar, stirring well.

Allow to cool before pouring into molds and freezing. After an hour, remove from the freezer and stir just to ensure that the mint is distributed evenly through the ice pops.

WATERMELON, ORANGE BLOSSOM, AND GINGER

1lb 10oz/750g watermelon flesh,
    roughly cut into chunks
4oz/120g crystallized ginger, cut
    into ¼ in/5mm cubes
1 tbsp orange blossom water
grated zest and juice of 1 lime
a measure or two of Cointreau
    give this an extra "dimen-
    sion"(optional extra)

So you've got fruit, fragrance, zing, and bite: what more could you want from an ice pop?

Blend (or pound) the watermelon, then whisk in the other ingredients. Pour into your molds and freeze. Stir after an hour so that the ginger does not all congregate at the tip.

Assabee bi Loz
FINGER BAKLAVA WITH ALMONDS

Baklava (*baklawa* or *paklava*). What's not to like? Pastry, honey, nuts. Goo, crunch, calories. Nearly everyone loves baklava: it's kind of addictive. Quite a few self-confessed diabetics come into my store to buy it, assuring us that they will just fiddle with their meds to compensate: this is very naughty, no?

Its origins are obscure, and as is often the case with culinary innovation, most Middle Eastern countries claim to have invented it. Although there are references to desserts made with fruit and pastry and nuts in ancient Mesopotamian texts, the concept as we know and love a bit too much was almost certainly created during the heady days of Ottoman culinary supremacy. Betcha didn't know that the Topkapı Palace employed a staff of up to 800 in its kitchens? Or that there is a town, Gaziantep, in southeast Turkey, that is so famous for its baklava that they say that when the wind blows in the right direction the aroma reaches Istanbul. Anyway, the Turks certainly grew very fond of the stuff, and even had an annual baklava parade (the *baklava alayi*) during Ramadan when the Sultan's troops were given trays of it to share.

Sugar was rare and expensive in antiquity, and so the first confections of this nature were made with honey or *pekmez* syrup.

There are perhaps eight or nine varieties of baklava, and to confuse matters each country gives them different names. I offer you this one (which is Levantine in origin), as it is by far the simplest to make.

Preheat the oven to 350°F/180°C and grease a baking tray.

Firstly, make the filling: mix the nuts, sugar, spice, and flower water into a paste.

Next, cut each sheet of phyllo into 4 rectangles, then cover them with a damp cloth so that they don't dry out. Take 2–3 phyllo rectangles at a time, and brush them with a little of the melted butter. Spoon a dollop of the nut paste on to one end of each rectangle, then roll the pastry away from you, tucking in the ends as you go. Arrange the fingers on the baking tray and brush the tops with the rest of the butter. Bake for around 25 minutes, or until a pleasant golden-brown color.

Meanwhile, make the syrup. Put the sugar, lemon juice, and water into a pan and gently bring to a boil. Turn down the heat and simmer for 2–3 minutes, then take off the heat. If you are using honey or fruit syrup, boil the water, add the honey/syrup, then take off the heat almost straight away, stirring well—otherwise the mixture turns bitter.

Allow the syrup to cool for around 30 minutes, then pour over the *assabee*.

Enjoy warm or cold. Perfect with coffee and even better with ice cream, *kaymak*, or crème fraîche on top.

MAKES ABOUT
40 LITTL'UNS

FOR THE *ASSABEE*:
9oz/250g roughly ground almonds (you could of course also use walnuts or cashews or pistachios or a mixture)
½ cup/3½ oz/100g granulated sugar
1 tsp ground cardamom (optional)
2–3 tbsp rosewater (or orange blossom water)
10 sheets phyllo dough (half a standard 14oz/400g package of frozen phyllo)
7 tbsp/3½ oz/100g melted butter

FOR THE SYRUP:
EITHER:
½ cup/12oz/350g superfine sugar
2 tbsp lemon juice
1¼ cups/300ml water
OR:
1¼ cups/300ml cups water
1¼ cups/300ml cups honey or *pekmez* or date syrup

Samboosah Hilwah
AISHA'S YEMENI SWEET NUT PIES

MAKES 50–60
BABY PIES

FOR THE FILLING:

1 cup/5½ oz/150g coarsely
    chopped raw cashew nuts
½ cup/2¾ oz/75g finely
    chopped raw almonds
½ cup/3½ oz/100g superfine
    sugar
1 tsp ground cardamom
1½ tbsp rosewater

TO MAKE THE
SAMBOOSAH:

10 sheets phyllo pastry (half a
    standard package of frozen
    phyllo)
oil, for frying
confectioner's sugar
    and ground cardamom,
    to decorate

Samboosah, sambosic, samosa: yup, it's all the same word root/kind of stuff—exotic pies, usually made to sell in the street. These are well-known Arabic street fare, although among my Somali and Yemeni customers they are most often cooked as comfort food, for a taste of "back home."

Aisha is half Somali, half Yemeni, incredibly beautiful and (considering she has four children under six) astonishingly serene. She is also a very good cook. Her English is getting better, but when she first came into the shop we used to have a lot of fun as she tried to mime the various spices she wanted. Remind me to show you the actions for fenugreek some time…

Mix the nuts, sugar, and spice together, then add the rosewater: the mixture should bind into a paste. If it still seems a little crumbly, add a splash of cold water.

Cut each sheet of phyllo into lengthwise strips: standard phyllo width is around 14¼in/36cm, so I usually aim for five 2¾in/7cm strips of each sheet. But you may do six 2½in/6cm strips. Cover the phyllo with a wet cloth so that it doesn't dry out while you're working. Lay one strip at a time on the work surface in front of you, short side facing you. Place a teaspoon of the nut mixture in one corner of the strip, then fold the pastry over so that the mixture is enclosed in a small triangular pocket. Next fold that triangle over, up the strip, then fold it back across again. Repeat all the way up to the top. Moisten your fingers with some water and squeeze the pastry edges together to seal. Do the same with all the strips.

Heat 1¼–1½in/3–4cm of oil in a heavy-bottomed pan (or use a deep-fryer with clean oil) until it is sizzle hot (but you don't want it smoking). Fry the pastries in batches, scooping them out once they are golden brown. Drain them on a piece of paper towel. Leave to cool a little before stealing one, as the center of these things gets really hot.

When cool(er), sprinkle with a little confectioner's sugar mixed with cardamom and serve with spiced tea or Arabic coffee. *Sahtein!* (Now you know how to say *bon appétit* in Arabic.)

I serve these with crème fraîche and some barberry coulis and they are excellent. What's that? You'd like my recipe for barberry coulis too? Oh all right then…

SNACKISTAN BARBERRY AND LIME COULIS

MAKES ¾ CUP/200ML
125g/4½ oz barberries, picked through and
    washed (or use redcurrants or cranberries)
1¾ cups/400ml water

2 tbsp sugar
juice and grated zest of 2 limes
1 heaped tsp ground fennel seeds
¾ in/2cm fresh ginger, peeled and chopped

Put the barberries in a pan together with the water and all the other ingredients. Bring to a boil and reduce by roughly half, stirring from time to time. Press through a sieve and cool. Drizzle over *faloodeh* (Persian noodle sorbet), or tarts, or anything you like really.

Booza

MASTIC ICE CREAM WITH PISTACHIOS

Booza is THE ice cream to eat in the streets of Arabistan, especially Syria, whence it hales. In some countries, it is actually sold as ice pops, in others it is served in paper cups. It's all kind of gloopy, like Indian *kulfi* or Persian *bastani*, and this is mostly due to the addition of *mastic* and *sahlab* (an orchid extract). As this latter is almost impossible to find (except as an ingredient in other things), I have substituted cornstarch.

MAKES ENOUGH
FOR 4 PEOPLE

3 tbsp cornstarch

3⅓ cups/750ml whole milk (oat milk works well too if you want a vegan version)

scant 1 cup/5¾ oz/160g sugar

⅓ tsp (i.e. 4–5 granules) mastic

1½ tbsp flower water (rose, orange blossom, or a mixture of both)

⅔ cup/3½ oz/100g chopped pistachios

2–3 tbsp fresh pomegranate seeds (optional: use fresh redcurrants or dried cranberries instead if you like, or just leave them out)

Put the cornstarch into a small bowl and add around 5 tablespoons of the milk, stirring well to get rid of any lumps. Pour the rest of the milk into a pan along with most of the sugar and warm gently. When it is fairly hot but not boiling, add a splash of the warm liquid to the cornstarch, mixing well once again, then tip the whole lot into the pan.

Next, pulverise the mastic with the remaining sugar (if you don't have a mortar and pestle, wrap it in a clean cloth, and bash it with your rolling pin) and add it to the hot milk along with the flower water. Bring to the point of boiling, stirring constantly, then take off the heat. Allow to cool completely before pouring into a suitable freezeable container (or your ice-cream maker if you have such a grand thing). Freeze for about 45 minutes, then take it out of the freezer and churn well. At this stage, stir in the pistachios and pomegranate seeds, then put it all back to freeze hard.

Remove from the freezer 5–10 minutes before serving decorated with more pistachios, or pomegranate kernels, or rose petals, or all three.

Dolmeh Shirin
DESSERT *DOLMEH*

In theory anything that is stuffed (we're talking cooking, not taxidermy: civet *dolmeh* would just be silly) can be called a *dolmeh*. So it kind of makes sense to extend this to the realm of sweet snacks too. Most importantly, the next three recipes are fun. And cooking is getting a little bit too serious, don't you think?

SWEET-STUFFED LETTUCE LEAVES

There are serious stuffed leafy things (usually vine leaves or cabbage leaves). And then there are these stuffed leafy things: romaine lettuce leaves wrapped around a fragrant rice and fruit stuffing served with date syrup cream.

Boil the rice until just cooked, refresh under cold water, and leave to drain for 30 minutes.

    Fill a bowl with really cold water and park it near your cooker. Next bring a pan of water to a boil and blanch the 30 pretty lettuce leaves a few at a time: they only need around 45 seconds. Remove them from the pan and plunge them into the cold water—this will stop them from becoming mushy and unworkable—before leaving them to drain in a colander. At this stage, drain the raisins and apricots as well.

    Tip the drained rice into a bowl and add the saffron together with the raisins, apricots, other spices, fruit, and nuts. Mix well.

    Take a lettuce leaf and put it on the work surface in front of you, stalky end pointing away from you. Place 2 heaped teaspoonfuls of the rice mixture at the end of the leaf nearest you, dot a tiny cube of butter on top, and roll the leaf away from you, tucking the side part in as you roll so that the filling ends up completely encased in lettuce. Repeat with the other leaves.

    Invert a plate (preferably not your best china) in the base of a heavy-bottomed pan, and scatter any substandard lettuce leaves across it. Arrange the *dolmeh* in a circle, working from the outside in, piling them up if necessary, and dot any remaining butter on top. Add the rosewater, *pekmez*, and lemon juice, then invert another plate on top. Add enough cold water to the pan so that you can just see it, and bring to a boil before turning down the heat and simmering gently. You will need to cook the lettuce leaves for around 15 minutes: once this time has elapsed, take off the heat and leave it somewhere to cool a little.

    Heat the cream gently in a small pan until it is just short of boiling, then take it off the heat and add the date syrup. Serve the *dolmeh* hot, warm, or cold with the sauce in a jug alongside. These are so good you might have to hide them from yourself.

MAKES 30

¾ cup/5½ oz/150g basmati (or long-grain) rice

30 nice romaine lettuce leaves (2 heads of lettuce), retain any less pristine leaves

⅓ cup/1¾ oz/50g raisins, soaked

¼ cup/1¾ oz/50g dried apricots, chopped and soaked

pinch of ground saffron steeped in boiling water

½ tsp ground cinnamon

½ tsp ground ginger

¼ tsp ground mace (or nutmeg)

3½ oz/100g dates, pitted and chopped

⅓ cup/1¾ oz/50g pine nuts (or sunflower seeds)

⅓ cup/1¾ oz/50g pistachio kernels, roughly chopped (or almonds, or hazelnuts)

5 tbsp butter, cut into pieces

2 tbsp rosewater

2 tbsp *pekmez* (grape syrup) or pomegranate paste

1 tbsp lemon juice

⅔ cup/150ml light cream

3 tbsp date syrup (or molasses)

CANDY STORE STUFFED TANGERINES

A TRICK TO PLAY
ON 12 CHILDREN

12 tangerines (or mandarins,
or clementines…)

½ small pineapple, peeled
and cut into small chunks

4 kiwi fruits, peeled and cut
into small chunks (of course,
you can use any fruit that is
not too soft)

½ tsp ground cardamom

juice of 1 small lemon

2 tsp orange blossom water

12 small pieces of *gaz* (Persian
nougat, but any nougat is
fine), cut into ½ in/1cm cubes

7oz/200g *halva*, cut into
½ in/1cm cubes

16 pieces of rose or orange
Turkish Delight, cut into
½ in/1cm cubes

2 small tubes of sour candy
powder like Pixy Stix (I also
found some under the name of
Rainbow Dust, which sounds
like it should be illegal)

Ameliaranne Stiggins* goes to Snackistan. These stuffed fruit are tons of fun, easy to assemble, and very popular with the under 10s and the over 23s. They are also pretty healthy, as after-school/party treats go.

Cut the top off each of the tangerines, and use a small pointy knife to prize the fruit away from the peel, taking care not to damage the latter. If the skin is baggy, then you can probably extract the fruit fairly easily with your fingers; if it is taut, then you will need to cut the segments out. Reserve the hollowed-out skins/tops and cut the tangerine pieces into chunks (removing any seeds along the way).

Add the pineapple and kiwi to the tangerine in a bowl. Mix the cardamom with the lemon juice and orange blossom water and pour it over the chopped fruit, mixing gently. Cover and set aside. Mix the nougat, *halva*, and Turkish Delight cubes in another bowl.

When you are ready to serve, put a little of the confectionery mix in the bottom of each tangerine, followed by a layer of fruit, followed by more cubes, and then top them with another layer of fruit (along with some of the juice). At the last minute, trickle some of the candy powder over each one, and recover them with the tangerine tops so that the fruit looks more or less whole. Keep a straight face as you serve them, reminding disappointed small people that in Ameliaranne's day tangerines were a treat. This one should earn you lots of bonus Wonka points.

Ameliaranne Stiggins and the Green Umbrella is a wonderful children's book written in 1920 by Constance Heward. The eponymous heroine, whose family is very poor, goes to a party and tries to bring back all of her food—cakes, tangerines, sweets—hidden in her umbrella to feed her ailing brothers and sisters. It made me think that maybe cakes and sweets hidden in a tangerine might be fun.

DATES STUFFED WITH SPICED *LABNEH*

MAKES 50

⅔ cup/5½ oz/150g creamed
labneh (or thick plain yogurt
blended with ½ tsp salt)

¼ tsp ground cumin

½ tsp sumac

¼ tsp ground cinnamon

¼ tsp red pepper powder
(optional)

50 dates (soft ones, such as
Iranian Bam or Medjool)

25 walnut halves (or 50 quarters)

So easy, but such a great thing to have in the fridge: they offer instant energy. I should warn you that this is the one thing that is never left over on *mezze* spreads, so set some aside for yourself from the beginning.

Blend the *labneh* with the spices, mixing well. Pit the dates, taking care to split them down one side only, and split the walnut halves. Fill each date with *labneh* and poke a walnut on top. Arrange prettily on a platter.

DESSERT *MEZZE*

You know how you often want everything on the dessert menu, and then you agree with your buddies that you'll each try something different and share it, and then they won't share with you? Or when you're having a little soirée and the conversation drops away because everyone is cramming cake into their mouths? Well, this idea gets around the problem. Throw everything in the middle and let them go wild. Share. Keep it informal. Keep the chatter going. Much better.

So what should you put on the table? The stuffed lettuce leaves and dates on pp.185, 186 are a good place to start. Readers of *The New Middle Eastern Vegetarian* will recall that I offered a recipe for sweet *houmous* made with *tahina*, honey, cinnamon, and cardamom. You can make something like *tsatsiki* by blending yogurt with honey, kiwi, or melon and chopped fresh mint. And a hot pepper fruit salsa (finely diced fruit dressed with rosewater, hot pepper, sugar, and lime) with sweetened mascarpone.

Fresh fruit for dipping is an obvious addition, but fruit or sweet vegetable chips are a lot more fun...

SNACKISTAN QUINCE CHIPS

MAKES ENOUGH FOR A PARTY BOWLFUL

¼ cup + 2 tbsp/2¾ oz/75g
    granulated sugar
1 tsp ground cinnamon
½ tsp ground nutmeg
½ tsp ground ginger
1 fat quince
    (around 10½ oz/300g)

You can, of course, use all kinds of fruits and veggies to make these sweet chips: sweet potato, beet, carrot, apple, pear, firm mango...

Preheat the oven to its lowest setting, and line a large baking tray or 2 smaller ones with parchment paper.

Mix the sugar with the spices. Peel and core* the quince and slice into very fine slices (with a mandoline if you have one), and spread them out over the baking tray(s). Sprinkle the spiced sugar over the fruit as evenly as possible, and bake for around 1½ hours, or until slightly browned and kind of crispy. Remove from the oven and peel off the parchment paper: the chips will get crisper as they cool.

Quince chips will keep for a few days in an airtight container.

* An Iranian housewife would retain the quince seeds as they are one of the best natural remedies for chesty coughs. Make a decoction of them, adding honey if necessary, and sip as tea.

SWEET *TABOULEH*

Salad is a must for most *mezze* spreads. You can always whip up a good fruit salad or you could push the *dhow* out and make a special sweet salad. This stuff hits the spot at practically any time of day and makes for a super-nutritious breakfast.

MEZZE FOR 8 OR
BREAKFAST FOR 4

5½ oz/150g assorted diced dried fruit (prunes,
    dates, figs, apricot, mango) or use diced
    fresh fruit (strawberries, banana, kiwi,
    pomegranate seeds, grapes …)
generous 2 cups/10½ oz/300g medium bulgar
    (cracked wheat)
1¾ cups/400ml very hot Earl Grey
    tea made with 6 tsp sugar
1 cup/5½ oz/150g assorted nuts:
    sunflower seeds, pumpkin seeds,
    hemp seeds, chopped pistachios, pine nuts

1 tbsp toasted sesame oil
2 tsp runny honey
1 tbsp raspberry vinegar
1 tbsp lime juice
big handful of fresh mint, shredded
big handful of fresh cilantro, chopped
few sprigs of fresh basil, chopped

If using dried fruit, soak for around 30 minutes then drain.

    Meanwhile, spread the bulgar out in a deep oven tray and pour the tea over it, stirring well. Cover with a clean paper towel or piece of foil and leave for about 10 minutes. At the end of this time, use a fork to fluff it up.

    When it has cooled more or less to room temperature, add the fruit and nuts, mixing well. Whisk the oil, honey, vinegar, and lime juice together and drizzle through the bulgar, checking that the "seasoning" (sweetness) is to your liking. Finally, stir in the chopped herbs. Prepare to amaze your guests.

 * Note

Wheat- or gluten-intolerant?
A very good *tabouleh* can be
made with millet, but you will
need to boil the grains in the tea
rather than just soaking them—it
will take about half an hour to
cook, and you will need to add at
least ½ cup/100ml extra water.

Something To
Wash It Down

Mullah Nasruddin took up his flask and went to the dairy to buy some milk.

"I'll have a choes *(just under 2 cups) of cow's milk, please, good man," he cried upon arrival.*

"Your container won't accommodate that much," replied the cowherd.

"Very well. Goats are smaller. Give me one choes *of goats' milk..."*

Snackistan actually has an impressive array of stuff to drink, including a wide variety of dairy derivatives: *ayran, kefir, doogh*… If you analyze it, the Middle East gave the West beer, wine, spirits, fruit syrups, drinking yogurt, and coffee, and tea, although that came via China. The West gave Snackistan soda pop. Doesn't seem quite balanced, does it?

Across Snackistan carbonated drinks are often sold, somewhat tellingly, by the color: orange, white, or black (this, I suspect, to avoid having to mention the corporate Western giants responsible for their creation). But in the streets and homes of the region, drinks are more likely to be homemade or freshly squeezed. I have cherry-picked some of the most unusual for your further quaffing pleasure.

ORANGE BLOSSOM AND MINT LEMONADE

**MAKES AN 8 CUP/
2 LITER JUG**

2½ cups/1lb 2oz/500g sugar

4 cups/1 liter water

3 tbsp orange blossom water

10 nice fat lemons

big handful of fresh mint,
    shredded

sparkling water (or still) to top up

mint leaves, lemon slices, and
    cucumber slices to serve

There is no excuse for buying that nasty artificial stuff that goes by the name of lemonade: the real thing is easy to make, even with a manual juicer.

This drink is a variation on the classic idea of *sharbat*, a sweetened fruit drink common to most Middle Eastern countries. The concept seems to have evolved in the seventh and eighth centuries, which is roughly when the advent of Islam put the kibosh on drinking more intoxicating beverages. Iced *sharbat* of one variety or another is available from street vendors all across Snackistan: particularly popular are quince, sour cherry, orange, and rose.

Our exotic lemonade has it all: a hint of floral sweetness, a soupçon of intriguing freshness, and a big hit of fragrant sharpness. Gosh: so many adjectives in such a small sentence. Without wanting to sound like a commercial for a second-grade supermarket chain any further, this drink packs it all for sweaty summer day refreshment. One glass is never enough.

Make syrup by boiling the sugar and water together. Once the sugar has all dissolved, add the orange blossom water and take it off the heat.

Next, scrub the lemons before zesting 5 of them and juicing all of them. Add both the zest and the juice to the cooling syrup. Once the mixture is quite cool, add the shredded mint to it, and put it in a covered container in the fridge to chill.

Serve it over ice in your prettiest ~~desperate~~ perfect-housewife jug, topped up according to taste with sparkling (or regular) water, and made irresistible with the finishing touches of extra slices of lemon, mint leaves, and cucumber. Stand back and marvel at your own domesticity.

BARBERRY JUICE

MAKES 2 CUPS/500ML

7oz/200g barberries
    (dried or fresh)

generous 2 cups/500ml water

2 tbsp sugar (optional)

This is real Persian street fare; to be honest, I've come across few Iranians who make it at home, and yet they all have childhood memories of drinking the stuff in sweltering summer streets and bazaars. There is apparently nothing quite like it for cooling the blood...

Barberries are astonishingly good for you: they are full of vitamin C and are used by herbalists to treat diabetes, renal problems (red stuff is generally good for the kidneys), and poor digestion. They grow all over the Middle East, Europe, and parts of North and South America, and feature in many Victorian English cookbooks (wherein they were mostly used to make jello).

This recipe was shouted at me by sundry tiny aunties-in-law all the way from Kermanshah (via Skype). Technology is occasionally a wonderful thing.

Pick through the barberries—they live up to their name and can be full of barbs and bits of twig—and wash them thoroughly. Tip them into a pan, add the water, and bring to a boil. Turn down the heat and simmer for around 20 minutes, then sweeten to taste and press through a fine sieve. Cool then chill until required—the juice should keep for up to a week.

KASHMIRI TAMARIND COOLER

Tamarind originated in India, and our name for it reflects that: the Arabs called it *Tamr Hindi* (Indian dates) as they weren't quite sure what it was at first. Indeed the tamarind is the Zaphod Beeblebrox of the fruit world: compellingly weird to look at, and full of surprisingly good stuff. It is famously cooling, packed with phytochemicals (the secret police of the nutrient world) and vitamins and trace minerals and fiber.

This recipe comes courtesy of my (Kashmiri) butcher's mother-in-law.

MAKES A GENEROUS 3
CUPS/750ML

10½ oz/300g block of tamarind (or use same weight of fresh, peeled pods,* or 2 tbsp tamarind paste)

generous 3 cups /750ml boiling water

juice and grated zest of 2 limes

¾ in/2cm piece fresh ginger, peeled and chopped

2 cloves

6 cracked peppercorns

2 cinnamon sticks

1¼ cups/9oz/250g brown sugar (traditionally jaggery, which is whole sugar formed into a cone)

Put the tamarind in a pan and pour the boiling water over it. Turn the heat on underneath the pan and continue to simmer gently, stirring from time to time, until the tamarind has more or less dissolved. Add the lime juice, zest, and spices, and cook for a further 10 minutes before turning the heat off and adding the sugar. Stir well and leave to steep for a further 20 minutes.

Next, press all of it through a sieve, pushing to get as much juice as possible from the pulp. Bottle the resulting syrup until needed.

Serve in brown-sugar-frosted glasses, over ice, topped up with ginger ale or soda water or just plain ol' water. Also reputedly "wicked" in cocktails (according to a local barman).

* Note on tamarind
Hmm... Pods. Well, you need to flake the outer husk away, then peel off the inner stringy stuff, and push out the seeds in the middle. The black gooey substance remaining is your edible tamarind. Handy hint: do not casually toss the seeds in the dying embers of an open fire: they explode (as do lychee stones).

Sharbat Amardine
APRICOT PASTE SYRUP

MAKES 4 CUPS/1 LITER
1lb 2oz/500g amardine (or
    the same quantity of dried
    apricots), cut into small chunks
4 cups/1 liter water
sugar, to taste

A lovely creamy fruity drink that works hot or cold. This is a comforting Ramadan special, made both at home and sold by street vendors, but to my mind it is far too good to be reserved for just one month a year.

Amardine is apricot fruit leather, and is available in most Middle Eastern stores now—but if you can't find it, just use good-quality dried apricots instead. Snackistanis make much of apricots, in tagines and stews, and using them dried in all kinds of creative ways. Try to find the Iranian variety known as *khaysi*, fresh or dried: the flavor is astonishing, like honey. I don't know what they are called in English, but just in case any of you are botany geeks, my Latin/Farsi horticultural dictionary gives the Latin name as *Armeniaca duhamel* (be very impressed).

Soak the amardine, preferably overnight.

Once the amardine has soaked for a goodly while, pour it all into a pan and bring to a boil slowly, stirring from time, until the mixture looks quite homogenized. If you are using dried apricots, a brief whizz in the blender would be beneficial at this stage. Add sugar (or honey) to taste; a squirt of fresh lemon or a splash of orange blossom water may also be added to lend extra oomph.

Enjoy hot (this rocks with a swirl of cream), or chill and have cold. I reckon amardine has good potential as a cocktail mixer, but at the time of writing this remains untried.

Karkade
HIBISCUS TEA

MAKES 4 CUPS/1 LITER
1oz/30g hibiscus flower
    heads/petals (fresh or dry)
4 cups/1 liter boiling water
honey or sugar, to taste

Hibiscus crops up all over the place: some nations call it roselle, while in my part of the world (Peckham) folks are more likely to use its Caribbean name: sorrel. But the country that can really claim it as its own is Egypt, and this drink's popularity goes back to the time of the pharaohs.

Regardless of whether they were actually aliens from another planet or not, those pharaoh guys really were pretty astute, as a lot of their favored comestibles are incredibly healthy. Hibiscus is full of antioxidants, but it seems to be particularly good for those with diabetes and high blood pressure.

Put the flowers in a pan or heatproof jug, add the water; sweeten to taste and leave to steep and cool for around 8 hours, or overnight. Strain and bottle. This will keep for a couple of weeks in the fridge. *Karkade* is most often enjoyed over ice in hot countries (kind of figures, yes?), but it is lovely as a hot drink. A word of warning—while you're admiring its deep red hue, remember that it stains…

FLOWER POWER:
ROSE, BORAGE, AND MARSHMALLOW TEA

Flower tea is nothing new. We've been drinking camomile and jasmine tea in the West for a long time. But this trio of teas is relatively unknown, rather pleasant, and comprises some potent pantry remedies in the mix. While these are not exactly street foods, they are doled out by *hakims* (or street doctors) in Afghanistan and Central Asia, and made all over the region as soothing medicinal compounds.

You can make flower tea from fresh or dried flowers, but it goes without saying that if you are using the former, find some organic ones if possible, or at least forage away from busy roads. You also need to make very sure you are picking the right thing.

Once you have sourced your petals, wash them in cold water then steep them in boiling water for around 8–10 minutes. A tea ball helps, but you can just make it loose in a mug or teapot. Strain the tea if you like, and add honey (or sugar) to taste.

Rose petal tea has a delectable aroma and a curiously fruity flavor. It is full of vitamin C, helps flush the kidneys, detoxes the urinary system, and reputedly soothes the nerves. Iranians drink it "to prevent coughs and colds."

Borage (*Borago officinalis*) tea is also good for winter snuffles, acting as a demulcent for stubborn coughs. It is also touted as a remedy for insomnia, depression, premenstrual syndrome (PMS), and anxiety.

Marshmallow (*Althaea officinalis*) tea—not to be confused with the wondrous, spongy candies on which we burn our mouths around campfires. Marshmallow has a pleasant flavor and packs a punch of goodness. It is a powerful demulcent, helping to relieve congestion on the chest and, um, down below. It is also said to be highly efficacious in the relief of sore throats.

Chai Karak
SPICED TEA

The word *chai* just means tea in most Indo-European languages, and so the rise of the term "chai tea" in the West causes much merriment, as it effectively means "tea tea" (in the same way *na'an* just means bread, and so "*na'an* bread" is "bread bread").

Anyway, the idea of drinking spiced white tea evolved during colonial times in India and kind of spread out from there. Arabs and Iranians are fond of black tea with cardamom, or bergamot, or rose petals, but most would not dream of adding such a heady mix as our recipe below, and the idea of adding milk to tea is quite abhorrent to them. But fancy tea bars in the bigger towns are starting to purvey fancy teas, and this spiced tea is already popular in East Africa.

Put the water and milk in a pan together with the spices and bring to a boil. Turn down the heat and simmer for 5 minutes, then stir in the tea and take off the heat. Cover the pan and allow to brew for a further 5 minutes.

To serve, fish out the cinnamon sticks and strain the tea into two cups, sweetening to taste. Slide one of the rescued cinnamon sticks into each cup and enjoy. Particularly good next to a roaring log fire, or in a candlelit bath.

TEA FOR 2

1¼ cups/300ml water

generous ¾ cup/200ml
    whole milk

½ in/1cm piece fresh ginger,
    peeled and grated

1 star anise

2 cinnamon sticks

6 cardamom pods, lightly crushed

4 peppercorns, lightly crushed

3 cloves

2 tsp loose black tea

sugar, to taste

ICED TURKISH DELIGHT COFFEE

A worried anxious person is a wretched person; he perishes away with grief. Let him drink our Effendi's coffee, let it intoxicate him, free him of his troubles...
(ascribed to Rumi)

The Turks take their coffee very seriously, but this recipe is more about frivolity and sweetness. It is just like regular iced coffee, but with a far darker heart. The drink hits you with its alluring aroma, and then caresses your tongue (did I just write that?) with exotic, fruity after-notes. Look: it's really good. And filling: a quaffable snack. Carob is an optional but delectable extra: blackstrap molasses or date syrup could also be used, or you could of course just use sugar.

MAKES 4 CUPS/1 LITER

20 cubes pistachio Turkish delight

5 Turkish coffee cups of water (about 1⅔ cups/375ml)

5 heaped tsp ground Turkish (or Greek) coffee

2–3 split cardamom pods

2 tbsp carob syrup (or use carob powder: see intro above and feature on p.202)

generous 2 cups/500ml milk (soy, rice, oat, or almond all work well too)

a big scoop of ice cubes (a generous ¾ cup/200ml)

Quarter the cubes of Turkish delight, spread out on a tray, and put it in the freezer for 2–3 hours.

Put the water in a small pan and add the coffee and cardamom, stirring well. Bring the liquid just to the point of boiling: as it starts to rise up the sides of the pan, take it off the heat (if you leave it beyond this the coffee acquires a burned flavor). Stir in the carob syrup and set aside to cool a little before straining through muslin (or some of that tough paper towel); a super-fine sieve will do in a jam. Add the milk, whisking well.

When you are ready to serve, wrap the frozen Turkish delight and ice in a very clean dish towel and beat the hell out of it (or use a blender if you possess a sturdy model). Tip the crushed ice into 4 glasses and top up with the coffee.

In winter: forget all that ice. Make the coffee/carob combo, strain it and add hot milk. Place a spoonful of chopped (non-frozen) Turkish delight in the bottom of each glass or mug, and pour the hot coffee over it. The *loukoum* doesn't exactly melt, but it does become wondrously gloopy. Serve with a long spoon and a smile.

A DUO OF SNACKISTAN SMOOTHIES

Smoothies are of course liquidized snacks: filling, nourishing, and because they're a drink, they can't possibly be fattening, now can they?

MOROCCAN AVOCADO SMOOTHIE

MAKES 2 GLASSES

1 large ripe avocado, skinned
　　and stoned
generous 2 cups/500ml milk
　　(almond works well here, but
　　any will do)
2 tbsp ground almonds
2 tsp orange blossom water
3 tsp confectioner's sugar
1 scoop ice cubes
slices of orange, to garnish
2 tacky paper cocktail umbrellas

I once trumped a very snotty head chef by producing avocado ice cream as a dessert (lowly sous chefs aren't supposed to be that creative). I paid for it in dish washing of course. The thing is, avocados are so creamy they just demand to be used in sweet recipes as well as savory.

　　This is not my invention but a well-established Moroccan drink.

Put the avocado in your blender (or chop it and then force it through a sieve) with a little of the milk and whizz until creamy. Add the rest of the ingredients and blend. Pour into two glasses, garnish prettily, and enjoy.

MELON AND ROSEWATER SMOOTHIE

MAKES 2 GLASSES

1 small ripe melon (Galia or
　　Ogen are perfect), peeled
　　and seeded
2 tbsp rosewater
grated zest and juice of ½ a lime
1 scoop of ice cubes
few dried rose petals, to garnish
　　(optional)

This Persian classic is a lovely free-from-everything recipe. Melons are eaten by the bucket in Iran in summer as they are naturally cooling. The West might just have discovered the marketable power of the smoothie, but Iranians have been making the things since forever.

　　While this makes a lovely drink as it is, I also like to freeze it so it becomes just solid and serve it as a kind of *semifreddo* to cleanse the palate between courses (only when I am showing off, of course).

Pop the melon in a blender along with the rosewater, lime, and ice and whizz until smooth-ish. Pour into two glasses and garnish with rose petals, if you like.

BONUS RECIPE: WATERMELON SMOOTHIE
You can also make an awesome watermelon smoothie by blending chunks of watermelon with raspberries, mint, lime, a hint of chili pepper, and pomegranate molasses.

ON CAROB

Most of you probably know that carob is used as a chocolate substitute, and that it grows in alien-looking pods. It is awesome: naturally sweet, and (dare I say it) with much more fragrance and taste than cocoa. It is also caffeine-free and full of calcium. I have always used carob syrup, which is widely available in Greek, Turkish, and Middle Eastern stores, but carob powder may be easier to source. Use it as a sweetener, or in marinades, salad dressings, and baking. Or mix with *tahina* (see p.120).

What a lot of you won't know is that the carob (which also uses the pseudonyms locust bean and St. John's bread) is also a notable little fellow because he gave us our unit of measurement, the carat: the Latin word (derived from Greek, like so many things) for him is *Ceratonia siliqua*. The carob bean is apparently consistent in mass, and thus came to be used as a weight for precious stones and gold.

Useless information of the day (because if you put all the useless information together it amounts to a life of dedicated geekery): Snackistanis are generally very fond of *faal* or divination, which can imply anything from horoscopes to palm-reading. The most popular method is the old Rosey tea leaves (and Kourosh coffee grounds). An astonishing number of our Cypriot and Middle Eastern friends practice it.

If you want to read your grounds, drink your coffee then invert the cup over the saucer. Wait for 5 minutes and peer at the results. Both the patterns in the cup and on the saucer can be "analyzed," and you should look for images both in the grounds and the spaces between them. An apple is a sign of achievement, birds and fish and trees are mostly good things, cats mean treachery, dogs fidelity, faces indicate change… Well, that's just to start you off. A lot of it is intuitive.

And by the way, the art of reading beverage dregs is collectively known as tasseography. You will thank me for telling you that one day.

index

bibliography

This is a list of books to which I refer constantly and keep in an untidy sprawl next to my desk: you will find a far more extensive list of recommended reading on the Snackistan website: www.snackistan.co.uk

FOOD

Claudia Roden, *A New Book of Middle Eastern Food* (London, Penguin Books, 1968)—the undisputed doyenne of Middle Eastern food writers

Helen Saberi, *Noshe Djan* (New York, Hippocrene Books, 1986)—remains unsurpassed on the subject of Afghan cooking

Margaret Shaida, *The Legendary Cuisine of Persia* (Northampton, Interlink Publishing, 1993)—the first lady to write a Persian cookbook in English

Rena Salaman, *Greek Food* (New York, HarperCollins, 1986)—in my opinion the best work on Greek food, sparkling with warmth and humor

Tess Mallos, *The Complete Middle Eastern Cookbook* (Hardie Grant Books, 1979/2012)—an astonishingly complete and authoritative round up, now delightfully back in print

Paula Wolfert, *The Food of Morocco* (New York, Ecco Press, 2011)—just a lovely, lovely book

Nevin Halici, *Sufi Cuisine* (London, Saqi, 2005)

HISTORY

Jean Bottero, *The Oldest Cuisine in the World* (University of Chicago Press, 2004)—proof that fine dining really isn't a new thing

Rodinson, Arberry and Perry, *Medieval Arab Cookery* (London, Prospect Books, 2001)—the most complete medieval work of reference on Arabic cuisine

[edited by] Sami Zubaida and Richard Tapper, *A Taste of Thyme* (I.B.Tauris and Co. Ltd, 1994)—a collection of fascinating essays on culinary history in the Middle East

HERBAL LORE

Dr. Sohrab Khoshbin, *Giahan Mojezegar* (Miraculous Herbs) (Tehran, Nashreh Salez, 2005)—this volume is in Farsi; the book is reputedly now available in English from the good doctor's Canadian website: www.drkhoshbin.com

V. Mozaffarian, *Dictionary of Iranian Plant Names: Latin, English, Persian* (Tehran, Farhang Moaser, 1996)

BY THE SAME AUTHOR

You know, just in case you've enjoyed this book...

Sally Butcher, *Persia in Peckham* (Prospect Books, 2007)—more of the same as this, but with a heavy Persian bias and a lot of anecdotes

Sally Butcher, *The New Middle Eastern Vegetarian: Recipes from Veggiestan* (Interlink Books, 2012)—a vegetable lover's tour of Veggiestan, twin state to Snackistan

WEBSITES

And finally a couple of really helpful websites...
For herbal lore and fancy plant names: www.pfaf.org

For its simply huge archive of articles on Arabistan and beyond: www.saudiaramcoworld.com

acknowledgements

A cookbook is a culinary autobiography, built over many years and through interactions with countless people, both chef-shaped and otherwise. It would be impossible to acknowledge all of those who have helped create it. But I will endeavor so to do nevertheless.

Firstly an enormous thank you to everyone at Anova Books, especially editress Emily Preece Morrison. The behind-the-scenes team are some of the loveliest people with whom I have had the pleasure to work: thanks are thus due to Yuki, the nice photo lady; Valerie, food stylist extraordinaire; Wei, for practically perfect props; Georgie, for brave and bold design; and last-but-not-least, Kom in PR. I am also indebted to Kathy, the copyeditor, for her i-dotting, t-crossing, and conversions.

I am indebted once again to my wonderful agent, Veronique Baxter, and her assistant Laura for their faith and patience.

I am also grateful to the team of loyal customers and friends who have tested, tasted, and tweaked the recipes, and from whom I have drawn inspiration.

I would also like to give special mention to my team of very supportive BFFs and fellow '63 babies: Caroline, Cathy, Fiona, Jan, Kate, and Lisette, not forgetting Claire and Russell —happy birthday year, guys.

Lastly: hugs and thanks to my (bestest supporter/sternest critic) mother, and my better half, Jamshid.

Sally
Peckham

First published in 2014 by

INTERLINK BOOKS
An imprint of Interlink Publishing Group, Inc.
46 Crosby Street
Northampton, Massachusetts 01060
www.interlinkbooks.com

Text copyright © 2013 Sally Butcher
Photography © 2013 Yuki Sugiura
American edition copyright © 2014 Interlink
Publishing Group, Inc.

ISBN: 978-1-56656-958-3

Library of Congress Cataloging-in-Publication data available

Commissioning editor: Emily Preece-Morrison
American edition editor: Leyla Moushabeck
Designer: Georgina Hewitt
Layout: Allan Sommerville
Cover Design: Julian D. Ramirez
Photographer: Yuki Sugiura
Home economist: Valerie Berry
Stylist: Wei Tang
Copyeditor: Kathy Steer

Printed and bound in China

NOTES
1 teaspoon = 5ml; 1 tablespoon = 15ml. All spoon measurements are level. Both metric and imperial measures are given for the recipes. Follow either set of measures, not a mixture of both, as they are not interchangeable.